To my ~~~ Steve ~~~

The Unforgettables

Legends are Unforgettables

Enjoy!

Chris Shumway

The Unforgettables

◆

People and Events of Cleburne County, Arkansas

Chastine E. Shumway

iUniverse, Inc.
New York Lincoln Shanghai

The Unforgettables
People and Events of Cleburne County, Arkansas

Copyright © 2007 by Chastine E. Shumway

iUniverse books may be ordered through booksellers or by contacting:

iUniverse
2021 Pine Lake Road, Suite 100
Lincoln, NE 68512
www.iuniverse.com
1-800-Authors (1-800-288-4677)

ISBN: 978-0-595-44633-9 (pbk)
ISBN: 978-0-595-70272-5 (cloth)
ISBN: 978-0-595-88958-7 (ebk)

Printed in the United States of America

This book is gratefully dedicated first to God who blessed me with angels on earth, my mother, Florence, and my father, Richard Lohman. They are my Unforgettables.

I dedicate this book to the people mentioned in this book and the ones behind the scenes who made my dream for this book a reality. I shall forever be obligated to each and everyone of you.

Florence Lohman   Richard Lohman

Contents

PREFACE

THE Unforgettables

This rich and colorful history book called 'The Unforgettables' is the story about Arkansans and events, which have made an outstanding difference in the Ozark Mountains. The impact of change and incidents on human lives and accomplishments made by these people and events added a vital dimension to historical understanding.

It provides high reading of literacy by dramatizing through drama, biography and articles making this story told in various ways. All of the people written about in this book are Christians and credit their success to just one of those things from God.

Cleburne County in the Arkansas Ozark Mountains has a colorful history. The 'Unforgettables' takes its readers on a journey launching on personalities and stories that have made this region so special.

There is a section about 'The inscrutable Land of Prim and its mysterious round boulders. It takes and acquaints readers to the history packed whisper of the community of Wilburn. It tells about Greers Ferry that was boomed by the completion of the Greers Ferry Dam and is now known as the 'sportsmen's paradise' nationwide.

On your sojourn journey you will meet people who have made an enormous difference in the building of Cleburne County. Some of the people you will become acquainted with in this book are; Johnny and Joyce Carlton, Fadylee and Cleta Davis, William Carl Garner, Geologists, Doug Hanson and Mike Howard, Rex Harral, Odis Hipp, Bess and WC Knapp, Lillie Stevens, Glynda Turley, Patti Upton, Greg and Dereta Wells, and many others.

Throughout the book are homespun true stories by incomparable Rex Harral, the last of the pioneers in Wilburn and Cleburne County. The book features a wealth of historic photographs, several which have not been seen before.

Unparalleled happenings in Cleburne County include: the disastrous falling of the historical Winkley Bridge and the March 15, 1984 tornado, which cut a swath through North-Central Arkansas destroying the Edgemont Bridge. The journey includes a respectful visit with President J. F. Kennedy at the dedication of the dam in Heber Springs, Arkansas. It tells about the Prim Centennial Parade with Governor Faubus and the study of the mysterious 'round boulders of California Mountain' by State Geologists Doug Hanson and Mike Howard. When you finish your pictorial journey throughout The Unforgettables book and meet some of the people who have made a difference and experience some of the events, the author is certain that it will be an Unforgettable remembrance.

THE PORTRAIT OF
WILLIAM CARL GARNER

For almost one-half of a century, Carl Garner's name has been equivalent with the integrity of the Greers Ferry Lake area. Carl Garner was instrumental in building the Greers Ferry Dam, which made a big difference in the lives of people and living in Cleburne County and the nation. His contribution to Cleburne County, Arkansas and the nation can only be appraised as complete successes; Carl Gamer has had a phenomenal life. Legendary and unpretentious 92 year old Carl Garner has made a difference not only in Arkansas but all over the nation. He has built dams and walked with Presidents. He has had a great impact, not only on the Greers Ferry Lake and the Little Red River Area but also on tourism and beautification in Arkansas and the nation. What William Carl Garner accomplished through his walk of life has set a new horizon for the enrichment of all mankind.

EARLY DAYS IN COLLEGE

Retired Carl Garner and his wife Jean live in a home overlooking the shores of Greers Ferry Lake in a small town called Tumbling Shoals, Arkansas. Carl has a son, Carl Wade Garner, who is an engineer, and Jean has two daughters, Donna Redding and Jeri Vangilder. His hobbies are photography, fishing, hunting, swimming and gardening.

William Carl Garner was born June 1, 1915 near Sulphur Rock, Arkansas. His parents were Burton (Bert) John and Minnie Pearl Morgan Garner. Carl was the eldest of three brothers, Charles, Lynn, Dean and a sister Lucille. His family lived on a farm in Independence County. They attended the Methodist church in Moorefield, Arkansas, their mode of transportation being a wagon pulled by two mules that were called Jim and Kate. Carl attended a one-room school through the 9th grade called Lone Oak School in Independence County Arkansas, where his father had also attended. His family raised cotton, wheat, corn, and sorghum as stable crops. They also had dairy cattle, hogs, a large garden and an orchard. During the Depression years, life was difficult, but the parents provided a close—knit and a loving Christian environment for their family.

At Christmastime, the Garner family piled into their mule driven wagon and rode to Batesville. This was an annual journey the family always looked forward to. His father would usually buy a stalk of bananas for about 75 cents from a railway car. The family could not afford to eat in a restaurant, but feasted on cheese, crackers and a stalk of bologna purchased at Barnett's Store. When Christmas day arrived, the children received candy, apples and oranges. Some of their presents were store-bought, such as clothes and shoes. Their mother made most of their clothes.

When the Depression hit in the 1930s, Carl and his brothers got up at daybreak to milk the cows. During the summer they worked in the fields until almost dark. Then at evening they milked the cows again. The boys learned to plow behind mules. Their father was a perfectionist when it came to straight rows and took great pride in his fine looking fields. If the boy's rows were not straight enough to suit their father, they would have to go back and plow them again. Carl is a perfectionist, carried over into his work throughout his career because of his father's teaching.

The Missouri Pacific Railroad track (later called Union Pacific) passed through the Garner property. A switch was located on their property, so the engine could pull the cars up a steep incline, one-half at a time. Having a train in the Ozark hills meant convenience, danger, history, romance and maybe opportunity for the hill people. When the Garner children felt the rumble of the ground and heard the blast of the distinctive train whistle they sometimes ran to watch the train highball down the track. Sometimes the Conductor threw the Garner children the 'funny papers' from the back of the little red caboose. The section of the freight train parked on the switch gave the hobos time to get off the train. They would go to the nearby Garner house and ask for food. Carl's mother always fed them, but if there was a muscular armed looking man, Carl's father would have him split a few blocks of wood in return for the meal. When the train pulled out to proceed to its destination, the conductor would throw flares warning other trains that might be coming from that direction.

In the fall of the year Carl, his brothers and their cousins enjoyed going quail hunting. At the time they had single barrel shotguns and one double barrel shotgun. Sometimes Carl would have to play dog as they walked and hunted in the fields.

The Garner children walked a half-mile to and from school. In the morning they waited for the neighbor children who lived farther down the road, so they could walk together. Carl first discovered his love for sports when he was very young. The family had a basketball goal on their farm and he and his brother concocted a baseball field for themselves. This was part of their social life, with fifteen to twenty children playing games, laughing and talking together. Their home was a popular place for the youth to congregate. It was common practice for the teacher to stay with one of the families. For two years, the teacher boarded at the Garners. Carl knew he had to be careful at school or the teacher would report him to his parents. He understood the standing rule of his dad. "If any of us got a whipping at school, we would get another one at home."

After the 9th grade, Garner went to Sulphur Rock High School and distinguished himself as a center on the basketball team. For the rural students, transportation was provided in the form of a pickup truck with benches in the back. Bows were placed over the truck bed and covered with tarps so the truck looked like a covered wagon, even to the gathered hole in the back. There were only dirt roads in the area. In the winter there was no heat, but the truck beat walking. Carl's mother died of pneumonia while he was in high school, making it harder for his father to get along with extra duties, but he always provided a way for the children to stay in school. Bert Garner was a role model for his children and many others.

Carl was known to have a zest for life. He excelled in sports and in the classroom. Carl's height and dexterity helped him become an outstanding basketball player at Sulphur Rock High School. The first year he played, the team won the county tournament. He was chosen for the valedictorian of his high school graduating class. At that time he was so shy that his brother, Charles, who was salutatorian, took Carl's place giving the valedictory address.

The first summer after graduation, he was working full-time on the farm when the basketball and football coaches at Arkansas College, who had seen him play many times, offered him an athletic scholarship. This was a dream come true. Upon entering Arkansas College Carl was soon to learn how poorly equipped and unprepared he was for the hallowed halls of learning. He soon realized he was not alone; there were others in the same position as he was.

Carl said, "Those caring professors and coaches, all saints to me now, together with the students, all such great friends, paved the way for me in the classrooms and in the sports arena."

During the first two years at Arkansas College, (later named Lyon College), Carl hitchhiked to and from Batesville every day, all 6'3" of him. During his junior year he lived with his Uncle Robert Garner doing farming chores. At that time his uncle worked in Batesville and provided Carl with transportation to college. He also picked up the college mail at the Batesville Post Office each day, sorted, and placed the mail in student's college mailboxes. Carl said, "Some of the other students at Arkansas College worked to make ends meet also."

When he was a senior he lived on campus in a college dormitory. He coached intramural athletics and officiated at high school basketball games in the college gymnasium to help finance his education. For each game he received seventy-five cents, and the college received the same amount also. He lettered in baseball, football and basketball. The college dropped football while he was there. Carl, whose number on the basketball team was always number 13, played center for the team, and was all state center in 1937. The team won the State Championship in 1938. This achievement earned the team the right to compete in the National Amateur Athletic Union's championship (now NCAA tournament) at Denver, Colorado. As a baseball pitcher, he was a leading player in this sport also. For two years he pitched against the future big leaguer Preacher Rowe, who was attending Harding College at that time. Local merchants frequently donated gas money for their travel to sporting activities. When they went to their destinations, they seldom stayed overnight because the college could not cover the expense.

While attending college, Carl said, "I learned to appreciate the value of time and friendships. 1 learned how to save and what a dollar meant. I did not drink or smoke, as I had a perception in my mind as to what I wanted to accomplish in my life but did not quite know in which direction God would lead me."

Garner looks back on his days at Arkansas College (now Lyon) with happiness and gratitude, and he appreciates the honors that his alma mater has awarded him. He has been inducted into the school's Athletic Hall of Fame, the Distinguished Alumni Award and was presented the Alumni Honorary Doctorate Degree from the college almost 60 years after he graduated. It was at College that Garner found his future professional career. He took a surveying course taught by John Morrow, Jr. and it changed his life. He became so competent that Morrow hired him during the summer. Charles Taylor, one of Carl's college friends, recalled that when Morrow was out surveying and couldn't make it to class, he arranged for Garner to teach in his place. Carl received his diploma June 1,1938.

Garner has said, "After four years at Arkansas College, I was ready to become a man. I had been exposed to the text and had absorbed some of it, but most importantly I had made hundreds of friends. 1 learned how to learn and I had a much greater love and respect for my family. I learned how to win and how to lose and learned the meaning of dedication, truth, and courage. Most important was I had a Christian background and Bible training. All of this knowledge has served as a foundation for building a career and a life that has been rewarding and satisfying to me."

Early Days in College Pictures

Lone Oak School -- Independence County Arkansas. Photo of students in 1908 which included Carl's father, second row on the left. Carl attended through ninth grade.

The Garner family from left: Charles, Lynn, Lucille, Dean and Carl.

CARL GARNER ... *Sulphur Rock, Arkansas*

Carl Garner is the priceless gift of Sulphur Rock, Arkansas, to the basketball world, having served four years on that team while in high school.

Garner is a senior in Arkansas College with one year in football, two in baseball, and four in basketball to his credit. This was Garner's second year as co-captain of the Panther Basketball Team.

With twenty-two years of experience, 180 lbs. of muscle, and 6 feet, 3 inches tall, Garner has all the makings of a man. He is recognized as the hardest worker on the team. His pet trick is robbing the ball under the opponent's basket. His position on the team is center and he was selected as All-State center for '36-'37.

Carl of Arkansas College (Lyon) in 1938.

From left, Carl's son Carl Wade, his wife, Carol, Carl and his granddaughter, Kirsten, attending Lyon College's 90th birthday party for Carl.

Sulphur Rock Arkansas School basketball team. Carl is second left of Coach Barnes. His brother, Charles, is fifth.

Arkansas College basketball team in 1938: Garner is front center, number 13, with trophy. Student coach Robert Lee Calaway in front row far left.

CAREER WITH THE U.S. ARMY CORPS OF ENGINEERS

As a result of taking the surveying course in college, Carl got his first real job with the U. S. Army Corps of Engineers. Fifteen days after graduating Carl went to work for the Corps, having later turned down an offer from the Ash Flat School District to coach there. He said, "After I went to work for the Corps, I knew that was where I wanted to be."

In his new position Carl was first assigned to help build levees near Pocahontas and Corning working for Project Engineer Bill Brodie. Later they repaired levees near Emporia, Kansas. In the early 40's Carl worked on seven rivers in the White River system staking out ten dam sites. Later he surveyed at Camp Robinson and for two new military air bases at Stuttgart and Newport, Arkansas. He also did field surveys for mapping of White River from Cotter to Batesville and Little Red River from Heber Springs to Searcy.

During World War II the US Government believed that if Hitler won in Europe he would attempt to invade the U. S. by way of Canada. The latest U. S. Government maps bordering Canada along Lakes Ontario and Erie were made in the 1800's and were completely out of date. The Buffalo New York District Corps of Engineers asked the Little Rock Corps to make new maps. Thirty Corps of Engineers including Carl and others on loan to the Buffalo District spent two years at Batavia, New York doing the field surveys for 37 new maps, including Niagara Falls, which were to be completed later in Little Rock. The winters were cold in New York. There was snow on the ground in the Buffalo area from October to March, sometimes 2 to 3 feet deep in places. Gasoline was rationed in New York. Carl was allotted 1 1/2 gallons per week for his private car.

Almost all of the farmlands from Batavia to Buffalo consisted of large orchards and vegetable fields. After the vegetables were harvested by machinery, there was an abundance of leftovers on the ground. The owner told the young surveyors to take what they wanted. Carl said, "We were gleaners and during the season we gathered plenty to eat. We spoke with a different accent but the people were very friendly which made the two years we spent there unforgettable."

The field surveys were completed in 1945 and Carl returned to the Corps Little Rock district office to assist in the completion of the defense maps. After the New York maps were completed, the Army Map Service asked the Little Rock District Corps of Engineers to prepare a map of the Japanese Island of Kyushu. The US Army was preparing to invade this island first within a short time. Carl said, "We then began working on a map of the island for an invasion by the United States. Our air surveillance photographs showed that the Japanese were burrowing into the sides of mountains and getting ready for any attacks. The photos also showed planes and other Japanese military equipment one-day, then rubble the next. American air attacks had destroyed them." The maps were on rush order and Little Rock staffed up to 900 people in order to meet the schedule. Carl's job was proofreader as the maps were being made. The invasion maps were almost completed when the atomic bomb was dropped. As soon as Japan surrendered the incomplete maps became history. The Little Rock District had a drastic employee reduction from 900 to 600 in 60 days and Carl was included in the layoff.

Carl then went to work for a private engineering firm in charge of mapping closed Army military bases in California, Alabama, and Kentucky. The Corps re-employed him in 1947 constructing levees and seawalls on the Arkansas River at Ft Smith, Arkansas.

In 1948 Carl Garner transferred to Mt. Home for the construction of Bull Shoals Dam and power plant. Due to housing shortage, the government built a government village for the employees. The dam was completed in 1952 and the power plant in 1954. At the time the dam was completed it was the 5th largest dam in the United States. President Harry Truman dedicated the dam in 1952. It was an unforgettable day for Carl who was honored to get to shake the President's hand. He also met the Governor, Sid McMath, Congressman Wilbur Mills and Senator John McClellan. He remembers that President Truman was wearing a snappy white suit and a white Panama hat on that sultry day. He also noticed as others did the pluck of this man. In his speech, he blasted the private power companies that had fought against the dams. President Truman spared no words against the private power companies for trying to stop building the dams. He said, "The fight for a general flood program had been going on for a long time. If it hadn't been for the New Deal and the Fair Deal of the last 20 years, you wouldn't have these dams and their improvements on these and other rivers like it. Put that in your pipe and smoke it."

After completion of Bull Shoals, Carl was sent to Branson, Missouri, for the construction of Table Rock Dam and power plant. Carl was Chief of a section in the Engineering Division. Branson was a small town with limited housing also. Carl and other government employees built their own homes. At that time the only show in Branson was the Bald Knobbers outdoors near the river. Table Rock was completed in 1959. The Greers Ferry project was next.

Lincoln Sherman, Resident Engineer at Table Rock wanted Carl to go with him as Chief of Engineering Division at Greers Ferry. Carl was reluctant to come to Heber Springs, but Sherman was persistent in his going there. Carl finally agreed.

Before going to Heber he worked in the District office in Little Rock for a short time on the government cost estimate for the Greers Ferry project. Carl came to Heber Springs in 1959 as Chief of the Engineering Division on the construction of the Greers Ferry Project. Even though Carl was reluctant to accept the Chief of Engineering position in Heber Springs, he soon knew where he would want to spend the rest of his life. Heber Springs was a wonderful place to live! With this demanding position as Chief of the Engineering Division he was in charge of engineering for the construction of the concrete dam and the power plant, two auxiliary earth dikes, the largest containing 2,750,000 cubic yards of material, relocating roads, constructing three bridges, relocating utilities, five towns, sixteen cemeteries, and lake clearing. He also met with dignitaries, individuals and groups regarding problems and procedures relating to the project construction. The first bucket of concrete was placed in April 1960. Workers streamed into the area to complete the dam. The last bucket of concrete was placed two years later. The auxiliary dikes were completed in

1963 and the power plant in 1964. The original government estimated cost of the Greers Ferry project was $63,000,000, and was approved by Congress. The actual cost was approximately $46,000,000. The Dam turned out to be one of Arkansas' architectural marvels at unbelievable savings. This was unusual for government projects.

As the Greers Ferry power plant was almost completed Garner applied for the position of Resident Engineer for the operation and maintenance of the Greers Ferry Project. He promised the Corps if selected, Greers Ferry would be the best project the corps had in the United States. He got the job, and for the next 34 years with his dedicated staff he did everything he could to keep that promise. With this demanding position came operation and maintenance of the dam, power plant and large auxiliary dikes and lake. Other responsibilities consisted of the development, construction, operation and maintenance of the lakes 15 parks with an annual visitation of over 5,000,000, visitor days, and visitor safety. He also oversaw the construction and operation of the Greers Ferry Visitor Center, now the William Carl Garner Visitor's Center, and three national nature trails. He formulated and managed the shoreline management plan. He originated the annual volunteer Greers Ferry Lake Cleanup and an Earth Day Event, In addition to the Greers Ferry Project, he was responsible for the enforcement of government rules and regulations for a 4,000 square mile area of the state, including 700 miles of streams and rivers, inspection of 55 miles of levees, and assistance in natural disasters. He was the primary spokesman and liaison with the public in the project area for disaster assistance and government operations. Carl and his staff received hundreds of awards and special recognition for the project. Carl said, "We believe we kept the promise as do others in the Corps of Engineers."

Career with U.S. Army Corps of Engineers Pictures

President Clinton after his Saturday address greeting Carl Garner. He then presented the president with an autographed painting of Iron Eyes Cody by Bob Timberlake.

U.S. Army Corps of Engineers Greers Ferry Dam and Lake completed in 1964. US Fish and Wildlife Trout Hatchery below the dam.

**U.S. Army Corps of Engineers Bull Shoals Dam located
on the White River near Mountain Home.**

**U.S. Army Corps of Engineers Table Rock Dam located on the upper White River
near Branson, Missouri. The US Fish and Wildlife Trout Hatchery is below the dam.**

DEDICATION OF GREERS FERRY DAM

During President Roosevelt terms. Congressman Mills went to his office several times attempting to get the Greers Ferry Dam project approved.

President Roosevelt would say, "Wilbur I know what you want. You want the Greers Ferry Dam, but you aren't going to get it." The 5th time Mills went into Roosevelt's office, the President said, "Wilbur I know what you want. You want the Greers Ferry Dam and you're going to get it." Later Mr. Mills also got the funding for the project.

Early in 1963 the Heber Springs Chamber of Commerce asked Congressman Wilbur Mills to assist in getting President Kennedy to dedicate the dam. Mills was largely responsible for getting the Greers Ferry project authorized in 1938. In 1963, Congressman Mills got a commitment from President John F. Kennedy to dedicate the dam in the fall. This was good news and planning began. Carl said, "Just getting the President to Heber Springs required a mountain of advance preparation." The Heber Springs Chamber of Commerce assisted the Corps of Engineers in the planning. The site for the dedication ceremony had to be cleaned, leveled, seeded, and watered for months. Several structures and a temporary bridge across the highway near the north end at the dam by the U.S. Army were built. Communication lines were installed and a luncheon tent was set up. Security fences were erected. The White House provided specifications for some of the structures.

About a week prior to October 3rd, Secret Service Agents from Washington came to Heber Springs. No stone was left unturned. It was imperative that the dedication site was ready and safe for President Kennedy's arrival and visit. Dave Grant, the Secret Service Chief, upon arrival said, "This is one of the most successfully planned and constructed dedication sites I have ever seen." Later Grant said to Carl, "The President only drinks water from Pennsylvania and you need to get some."

Carl said, "With only two days left until the President comes I do not know how this can be done."

Mr. Grant said nothing in reply to this statement.

On the morning of October 2nd, Grant told Cart to take the white Lincoln Convertible, which had been stored in Carl's basement for about two weeks and have it washed. The car was on loan from a dealer in Memphis, Tennessee for the President to ride in. Grant said, "You stay with it the full time." Then he said, "You get Cokes for the President.'

Carl replied, "I will get the Cokes, and you get the water."

He said, "Okay."

The day before the President arrived, Mr. Grant asked Carl to give him a list by 2:00 P.M. of workers, private and government men and women, who might need to be in the area near President Kennedy. Carl was hesitant to take on this responsibility, "but Grant insisted I do it, and I did."

Grant gave Carl silver lapel pins for each of the men and women on the list to wear. The list of names was forwarded to the Washington Secret Service office for a security check, which was approved.

The day of the dedication, October 3, 1963, the Arkansas National Guard, including the local unit and the US Army provided security on site and along the travel routes. President Kennedy flew from Washington to Little Rock Air Force Base on *Air Force One*. Then he traveled to Heber Springs by *the President's helicopter* along with two others. The Corps of Engineers had constructed a grass heliport for Kennedy to land one-forth a mile west of the dam. The speaker's platform was built so that the dam and lake would serve as a backdrop.

The President arrived at the dam site about 10:45 a.m., and stayed until 1:35 p.m. The President and party first stopped at the overlook to view the dam. The Corps Division Engineer, General Dunn and Carl were waiting at the overlook. Describing that day, Carl said, "General Dunn told me that Senator Fulbright would introduce him to the President, and then he would introduce me. General Dunn was introduced, but he forgot me. Later Senator Fulbright introduced me."

The mayor had declared the day a citywide holiday. Businesses closed their doors. More than thirty school buses from local schools carried people from parking areas located south of the dam to a designated unloading site. Then the people walked across the Baily Bridge to the dedication site. A reserved section included 1,200 chairs, while another 5,000 were arranged for the general public. Carl was honored to sit on the speaker's platform with President Kennedy along with two distinguished senators, J.

William Fulbright and John L. McClellan, and Congressman Wilbur Mills (in whose district the dam was located), Oren Harris, Jim Tremble, E. C. "Took" Gathings, Governor Orval Faubus and other dignitaries.

President Kennedy was very tanned and wore a blue shirt. He hugged Mill's mother on his way to the speaker's platform. Senator John McClellen introduced the President.

In his 15 minute speech, the President Kennedy acknowledged, "... pound for pound, the Arkansas delegation in the Congress of the United States wields more influence than any other delegation of the 49 states."

Kennedy also noted that Wilbur Mills had just helped the administration pass an important tax bill. According to the President, *The New York Times* said, "If Congressman Mills suggested it, that the President would be glad to come down here and dedicate this dam and sing *'Down By The Old Mill Stream'* ... and I would be delighted."

In President Kennedy's speech, he challenged those people who said it is a 'pork barrel'. He said, "which is more wasteful—a multi-purpose project which can be used by all of our people-which is more wasteful, to fail to tap the energies of that river, to let that water flood, to deny this chance for the development of recreation and power, or to use it and to use it wisely? Which is more wasteful—to let the land wash away, to let it lie arid or to use it and use it wisely and to make those investments which will make this a richer state and country in the years to come?"

After the speech President Kennedy greeted the crowd. Several bands, including the University of Arkansas marching band and singing groups, including the Arkansas University Scholar Cantata and the Arkansas College Lasses, skydivers and Miss Arkansas, Pamela Jackson, provided the entertainment from 8:30 until 11:31 when Kennedy was to speak.

In addition to his speech the President joined hundreds of people who had paid for the luncheon. Tickets for the boxed barbecue/chicken lunches were $3.50 for adults and $1.75 for children prepared by the Batesville Young Men's Business Club. The boxed lunches included a white souvenir napkin inscribed in gold letters: "I ate lunch with JFK at Greers Ferry Dam."

Earlier Dave Grant informed Carl that he would ride in the President's car from the speaker's platform to the luncheon tent and then back to the helicopter. After the dedication ceremony was over, and Carl started towards the car, Mr. Kellerman, head of the Secret Service asked him where he was going. Carl said, "To ride with you to the luncheon tent."

Kellerman said, "No you are not."

Carl pointed to Dave Grant who was nearby and said, "Dave said I should."

In a rather commanding voice, Kellerman said, "Get in." Carl sat in the front seat between him and the Secret Service driver. President Kennedy, Governor Faubus and Wilbur Mills were in the back seat. On the way to the luncheon tent, Garner told Mr. Kellerman he was also to ride to the helicopter and would there be a problem.

Kellerman said, "I know you now."

On the way back to the helicopter they rode through the Dam Site Park where they viewed the sailboats that came down from Fairfield Bay to greet the President. While riding, President Kennedy said, "Turn on the radio, let's hear what the World Series baseball game score is."

As they neared the park exit the local Arkansas National Guard Soldiers were standing at attention. Mr. Mills asked Carl for the name of the Commander. He told him Richie Lee.

The President said, "Stop the Car." He then got out and shook hands with many of the unit. Later a young man who was at the end of the line said his knees were shaking so that if the President had gotten to him he might have fainted." The President then boarded the helicopter and with a smile waved goodbye.

NOTATION: Carl said: "Dave Grant gave me a gold p.t. boat tie clip, and, I received an autographed picture of the President about 2 weeks before he was assassinated."

The Greers Ferry Dam Dedication was one of President Kennedy's last major public appearances before his assassination. It was the saddest day of the nation in losing the revered President, but Arkansans know that he will always live on in their hearts and the honored day of the Dedication of the Greers Ferry Dam will never be forgotten. Carl said, "America cried and I cried."

Ceremonies commemorating the October 3rd, 1963 dedication of Greers Ferry Dam by John F. Kennedy were held on the 20th, 25th and 40th anniversaries at the dedication site.

Dedication of Greers Ferry Dam Pictures

The October 3, 1963 Dedication of Greers Ferry Dam by President John F. Kennedy. Platform guests include Senators John McClellan, J.W. Fulbright, Congressmen Wilbur Mills, Oren Harris, E.C. Gathings and J.W. Trimble, Carl Garner and 62 other guests.

Mr. R. H. Taylor	Mayor Floy Berkowitz	Dr. J. W. Jackson	Judge John Johnson	Mr. Truman Baker	Mayor James Huntly		Miss Hochfalbeimer	Miss Pamela Jackson	Maj. Jack Montgomery	Mayor B. R. Morse	Brig. Gen. M. A. Bywater	Mr. Fred Livingston
Mr. Dalton Sullivan	Mr. William Apple	Mr. Wayne Hampton	Dr. Claude Barnett	Col. John Morris	Mr. William Kennedy		Judge J. C. Crabtree	Mr. Lincoln Sherman	Mrs. R. E. Weaver	Mr. Walter Aldridge	Dr. David Mullins	Mr. Cliff Pearson
Mr. John Morrow	Sen. Greason F. Nixon	Rep. Cecil Alexander	Mr. Harry Oswald	Mr. Patrick Black	Mr. Carl Williams		Rep. M. N. Evans	Mr. Gerry Shupe	Mr. W. M. Shepherd	Mr. John Riggs	Col. Stounton Brown	Mr. Carl Garner
Mr. Roy Medlock	Mr. Arlo Taylor	Ex. Cong. Clyde Ellis	Mr. James Clendening	Mr. Herbert Thomas	Col. C. C. Maynard		Maj. Gen. T. H. Sanford	Maj. Gen. S. T. Clinger	Mr. Douglas Wright	Mr. Reeves Ritchie	Mr. Leonard Young	Mr. T. S. Cook
Rev. Walter Hill	Cong. M. J. Kirkade	Brig. Gen. E. H. Dooie	Mr. Tom Harper	Mr. Roy Kettnecken	Gov. John Dathoi		Mr. Tom Direstead	Cong. John E. Fogarty	Cong. E. P. Boland	Judge Pat McNally	Gov. Kim Babcock	Rev. William Wilder
	Lt. Gen. Walter Wilson	Sen. J. W. Fulbright	Gov. O. E. Faubus	Sen. John McClellan	Pres. John F. Kennedy		Cong. Wilbur Mills	Mayor W. J. Allbright	Cong. Bren Hance	Cong. E. C. Gathings	Cong. J. W. Trimble	

Seating Arrangement Platform

PODIUM

Name of people sitting on the speaker's platform.

President's limousine. In back seat is President Kennedy, Congressman Mills and Governor Faubus. Front seat is Garner and two Secret Service agents.

The crowd including the Arkansas University Band and Choir, US Army Band, Arkansas College Lasses Choir and others.

The president and congressional delegation arriving at the heliport south of the dam.

General Dunn greeting president on arrival at the dedication site.

President viewing Corps of Engineers Arkansas River lock and dam model.

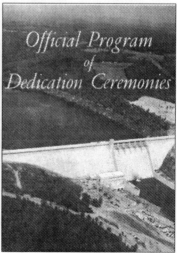

Dedication program cover.

President Kennedy visiting and shaking hands with the people.

Bronze bust of President Kennedy located in Kennedy Park at the site of the dedication.

President speaking to Secret Service agent.

25th anniversary ceremony commemorating the October 1963 dedication of Greers Ferry Dam by President John F. Kennedy. Congressman Bill Alexander is at the podium.

The Metropolitan Museum of Art

Fifth Avenue at 82nd Street, New York, N.Y. 10028   212-TR 9-5500

Sept 22. 1983

Dear Mr. Garner,

Again, thank you so much for your kind invitation. I am sorry I won't be able to be with you. As I mentioned, it really means a lot to my family when my father is remembered and honored as he will be at your ceremony. I hope to see Greer's Ferry Dam someday soon —

Best wishes

Caroline Kennedy

Caroline Kennedy's reply to invitation to the 25th anniversary ceremony of President John F. Kennedy's dedication of the Greers Ferry Dam.

THE GREERS FERRY LAKE & LITTLE RED RIVER CLEANUP

By 1970, Greers Ferry Lake had been filled for six years, and the public came by the millions to play, camp, boat, fish, swim and sightsee. Tons of litter was scattered and left after their visits. The Greers Ferry Corps of Engineers office did not have enough funds to clean the entire area.

Resident Engineer Carl Gamer set in motion a public volunteer program to clean up Greers Ferry Lake and Little Red River. Some doubted that this could be accomplished on a 31,500-acre lake with 276 miles of shoreline, and 20 miles of Little Red River. Gamer began by contacting the Greers Ferry Lake and Little Red River Association and other community and state leaders and by putting in hours of time and hard work.

The first Cleanup was held in late September 1970. Inclement weather limited participation to about 100 volunteers, but the job was started. This was an unforgettable historical event. From that moment on the Clean Up project was co-sponsored by the Corps of Engineers and the Greers Ferry Lake and Little Red River Association. It was then scheduled as an annual event for the first Saturday after Labor Day in September. A plan was completed with six objectives:

*Removal and reduction of litter by volunteer effort.

* Involve as many people as possible.

*A continuing educational program.

*Instill a sense of pride & ownership in the nation's public lands.

*Recycle resources.

*Provide a model for others.

By 1980, volunteers numbered more than 3000 people. This included 1200 Scouts, school groups, various civic clubs, oldsters and youngsters. Pontoon boat owners volunteered 120 boats to transport volunteers to assigned Cleanup areas on the lake. For the river Cleanup, the marinas and scouts provided boats and canoes.

Financial and in kind support numbered more than 300 donors. Some major contributors included, Coca-Cola, Miller Brewery, Aromatique, local banks, Arkansas National Guard, the Keep Arkansas Beautiful Commission, lake and river Marinas, motels, Cranford, Johnson, Robertson and Woods and local and state news media.

The entire 276 miles of lake shore and 20 miles of river were cleaned from 8 a.m. to 12 noon. Adopt A Highway volunteers also cleaned many miles of state highways on this historical day.

Participants were issued two types of plastic bags. One was for trash to be disposed of in the local landfill and one for aluminum cans to be purchased by a recycling company. One year about 8000 pounds of cans were purchased (not all from Cleanup). The trash was disposed in a local landfill. At noon on Cleanup day, a visiting VIP and press luncheon was held at the Red Apple Inn on Eden Isle. Mr. Win Rockefeller sponsored the luncheon for seven years. About seventy-five people attended by invitation only. As Master of Ceremonies, Gamer extended a welcome to the Cleanup thanking everyone for their participation and support. He also presented Cleanup Hall of Fame awards to eligible participants.

After the luncheon, everyone went to the Narrows Park to enjoy the musical entertainment. Cleanup volunteers came to the Narrows Park for a free catfish lunch and live entertainment by several groups and bands. One year 1900 pounds of catfish was cooked by volunteers and served by Heber Springs school students. More than 3,000 people showed up and enjoyed an afternoon of entertainment. Some of the entertainers over the years were Lyon College Pipes and Drums, Harding University Choir, Union Pacific Railroad band. Local Retreads, Jeff Smith and Ronnie Stoneman bands Hee Haw, Tom Grant and Lisa Stewart Bands, Nashville, Tennessee, Jo Ann Castle of the Lawrence Welk Show, Louise Mandrell, Jimmy Driftwood, Grandpa and Ramona Jones and Family, Jim Ed Brown and many others.

VIP's attending included Iron Eyes Cody, Astronaut Mike Lounge, Governor Bill Clinton and Hillary Clinton, Senators David Pryor and Dale Bumpers, Congressman Bill Alexander, Roger Power President, Keep American Beautiful and staff, officials of the Corps of Engineers and the Arkansas National Guard, press, radio and TV stations. The success of the Volunteer Cleanup Program prompted Mr. Al Pollard and Gamer to promote the Great Arkansas Cleanup, started in 1979, which included all

Corps of Engineers lakes in Arkansas and the Arkansas River using the Greers Ferry Program as a model.

Senator Dale Bumpers attended the Cleanup activities and was so enthused with the volunteer Cleanup idea that he introduced legislation, using Greers Ferry as a model. In 1985 Gamer testified before the U. S. Senate Subcommittee on Energy and Natural Resources about the success of the local effort.

Congressman Bill Alexander sponsored the legislation in the House of Representative's which became Public Law 99–402 the Federal Lands Cleanup Act of 1985, requiring all federal land management agencies to organize and conduct similar volunteer Cleanups the Saturday after Labor Day each year. This law also required the President to issue a proclamation to urge all people to participate in the Cleanup.

After the hearing and the bill became law. Senator Bumpers wrote to Carl saying, "One of the most gratifying days I have spent in the Senate was March 4, 1985 when you testified in behalf of the Federal Land Cleanup Act."

In 1996 Senator Bumpers by Public Law 104–333 changed the name to the Carl Gamer Public Lands Clean up Day. The Greers Ferry event has attained national recognition by winning 21 national awards and numerous state and local awards. It is a total volunteer effort requiring commitment and determination from thousands of people dedicated to keeping our resources clean and natural for future generations to enjoy. Millions of volunteers, nation wide, now Cleanup Public Lands saving the Federal Government millions of dollars each year.

Greers Ferry Lake and Little Red River Clean Up Pictures

From left, Carl, Billy Lindsey, and George Purvis, promoting the Lake and River Cleanup on Purvis "Arkansas Outdoor" show on KARK TV.

Ross Moore, Greers Ferry Lake and Little Red River Association, at a lake and marina check in station assigning cleanup location for Carmie Henry to transport group on his pontoon boat to the area.

Returning with bags of trash.

Group placing bags of trash in National Guard truck to take to landfill.

From left: Col. Bonine – Little Rock Corps of Engineers District Engineer, General Robinson SWD Corps of Engineer Division Engineer and Carl Garner Greers Ferry Resident Engineer with bags of trash collected.

Scouts returning with litter collected on lake shore.

Dr. John Zirschky, acting assistant to the Secretary of the Army Civil Works, (second from right with bag) Carl Garner and Scout Troop 78 of Memphis, Tenn.

Three young volunteers cleaning the lake shore.

Diver cleaning the lake bottom.

Heber Springs High School Charisma Club returning with bags of trash.

Chuck Dovish interviewing Carl Garner
about success of the cleanup.

Bill Lindsey, owner of Rainbow Resort and Trout
Dock, with cans retrieved from river bed with
long handled retriever.

Cleanup group with litter collected on road-
way near the lake.

Scouts preparing to clean up on the Little Red River.

Photo of nine astronauts made in space and autographed by each and with note to Garner. Mike Lounge, one of the astronauts, attended the cleanup one year. The note to Garner reads: "To Carl with thanks for making your part of the earth as beautiful as it all looks from space. STS 35 Crew"

Coca Cola buying aluminum cans at the Narrows Park collected by volunteers in lake and river for recycling. Volunteers received the money.

Carl Garner:

A man with an idea that captured the imagination of the nation

Carl Garner checking various types of trash at local landfill.

Cleanup patches Scouts -- Explorer, Boys, Girls, Corps of Engineers -- for cleanup participants -- Keep Arkansas Beautiful, special by Keep Arkansas Beautiful Commission.

Carl Garner and Iron Eyes Cody, the media person for Keep America Beautiful for many years. He attended the Greers Ferry Lake and Little Red River cleanup three times.

Garner welcomes and thanks the group for support and attendance. From left: Ramona Jones, Jeff Smith, Laverne Feaster, Jerry Atchley, and Dr. John Griffith.

Senator Dale Bumpers speaks to the group including former Governor Sid McMath and Garner.

Garner welcomes and thanks a later year group.

Greers Ferry Lake and Little Red River Clean Up VIP
and Press Luncheon

Garner presenting the Cleanup Hall of Fame award to Lindy Bowie of Coca Cola Co.

Rollie Remmel presented a Rollie Stick to Col. Scott Morris.

From left: Astronaut Mike Lounge, Grandpa Jones and Garner at luncheon.

Garner presenting the Corps of Engineers appreciation award to Iron Eyes Cody.

Garner presenting Cleanup Hall of Fame award to Cliff Peek.

Volunteers enjoying the entertainment.

From left: Al Pollard, Roger Powers, president of Keep America Beautiful, and Tom Olmstead, emcee.

Senator David Pryor and Congressman Bill Alexander.

Crowd enjoying hot air balloons.

Carl Garner, Jeff Smith Hee Haw, Jean Garner, and Hillary Clinton.

Carl Garner and Win Rockefeller, honorary chairman of Great Arkansas Cleanup.

Greers Ferry Lake and Little Red River Clean Up Free Fish Fry and Entertainment

Grandpa and Ramona Jones and band.

Jim Ed Brown and band.

Louise Mandrel.

Jo Ann Castle of Lawrence Welk show.

Lyon College pipes and drums.

Harding University Choir.

The Great Spirit Prayer

Oh Great Spirit whose voice in the winds I hear
And Whose Breath gives life to all the world-
Hear me.
Before You I come, one of Your many children.
Small and weak am I.
Your strength and wisdom I need.
Make me walk in beauty.
Make my heart respect all you have made.
My ears to hear Your Voice.
Make me wise that I may know all You have
taught my people.
The lessons You have hidden in every rock.
I seek strength, not to be superior to my brother.
Make me able to fight my greatest enemy -
myself.
Make me ready to stand before You with clean
and straight eyes.
When life fades, as the fading sunset, may our
spirits stand before You without shame.

Iron Eyes Cody giving
the Great Spirit prayer.

Hillary Clinton speaking to crowd.

Jimmy and Cleda Driftwood.

Senator Dale Bumpers visiting with scouts.

THE WILLIAM CARL GARNER VISITOR CENTER STORY

In the early 80s, public visitor centers were being constructed at several Corps projects. Carl Garner thought there should be one in Cleburne County. In the annual budget it was requested a sum of $100,000 to design and prepare plans for a visitor center. For five years the District deleted it. Carl Garner decided to go through a friend in the Division office to restore the funds in the budget, and the center was designed. Later, Congressman Alexander added $400,000 to the Greers Ferry budget to start the center. He later called regarding status of the Center. Carl informed him that the Corps Division office planned to use the money in Texas.

One of the Corps Division employees told Carl that this Center would be built over his dead body. Congressman Alexander then asked Carl how he could assure the funds would be used for the visitor Center. Carl said, "Include wording in the legislation that the $400,000 would be used only for construction of the center." Alexander had the bill passed, and 30 days later the project was advertised for bids. When the center was completed in 1983, Congressman Alexander wanted to name it the Carl Garner Visitor Center, but Carl objected.

Approximately ten years later Alexander informed Carl that it was being renamed the William Carl Garner Visitor Center. Carl again questioned this but Public Law 102–580–1992 had already changed the name. Carl said, "This was an immense honor for me."

William Carl Garner Visitor Center Story Pictures

Congressman Bill Alexander by act of Congress changed the name of the Visitor Center, is speaking at the name change ceremony. Other platform guests from left: Master of Ceremony Dr. John Griffith, president of Lyon College; Col. Ruff, District Engineer, Corps of Engineers Little Rock District, Carl Garner, Senator Dale Bumpers, Miss Arkansas Sharon Boy, Senator David Pryor and Reverend Bill Womack.

Unveiling of the new plaque from left, Congressman Bill Alexander, Senator Dale Bumpers, Carl Garner, and Senator David Pryor.

Carl Garner speaking.

Beginning with second person from left: Congresswoman Blanche Lincoln, Senator Dale Bumpers Jean Garner and Jack Murray.

Aerial photo of the center.

Corps of Engineers Castle and name of center located near the entrance.

THE EARTH DAY PROGRAM

The first Earth Day was held in April 1970 and was so successful that it started a national environment movement. It was the largest organized demonstration in history. Congress adjourned for a day and hundreds of ecology fairs were held.

In 1990 Garner decided the Greers Ferry Corps of Engineers and many other participants would be a part of the 100 million people worldwide Earth Day celebration. The first event was held at the Garner Visitor Center from 1 to 5 p.m., April 22, 1990. The event included more than 20 exhibits and hundreds of visitors including Congressman Bill Alexander, 2 state representatives and other dignitaries. By 1992 the Greers Ferry Earth Day was the largest in Arkansas and remained so for a number of years. It was labeled a huge success by the Cleburne County Times with attendance estimated at more than 2,500 which included 1200 school students. The 30 exhibitors from around Arkansas and Tennessee had displays making environmental education available on such topics as solar energy, soil conservation, wildlife, a large fish aquarium and many others. A pre Earth Day poster contest was held in 22 schools with 4300 students participating. Winners were awarded at the Earth Day program. Woodsy Owl, Smoky Bear and Resource Raccoon, school group skits, guided trail and power plant tours were part of the event. A formal program at the outdoor event featured a number of dignitaries supporting the program. Some of them were State Representatives Randy Thurman, Tom Collier, Bill Mills and Senators Stanley Russ, Steve Bell and Alan Gordon, United States Congressman, Wilbur Mills and Bill Alexander, Director Arkansas Parks and Tourism, Richard Davies, and Miss Arkansas, Heather Hunnicutt. Each Speaker had a special message with one theme through education of our young, dedication to our goals and with each of us doing our part we can change the course of our destructive habits and keep our earth the way God intended for all generations to come. The program ended by a delightful performance by Grandpa Jones and his band.

At the time Heber Springs Mayor, Ed Roper said, "This is one of the best education programs I've seen on saving the earth. What our kids learn about the environment today will make all the difference in what shape the world is in tomorrow. Garner and his dedicated staff appreciated all who participated for making this Earth Day one of the best in the nation." He continued saying; "You can make a difference. We can change the earth if we change our habits. Let earth have its day. Make Every Day Earth Day!"

Carl retired in May of 1996 with 58 years of service with the Army Corps of Engineers. Carl made his home on Greers Ferry Lake near Heber Springs where his treasured memories began.

The Earth Day Program Pictures

Earth Day supporters and participants including Congressmen Wilbur Mills and Bill Alexander, State Senators Steve Bell and Allen Gordon, Jerry Atchley, Randy Thurman, Carl Garner and Miss Arkansas Heather Hunnicutt.

Local post office provided special Earth Day commemorative postal cancellation.

Congressman Alexander addressing the crowd along with others.

Congresswoman Blanche Lincoln greeting one of the exhibitors.

Donna Glascock, manager of the Visitor Center, with poster contest winners.

Congresswoman Blanche Lincoln, Garner, and others viewing the Arkansas Game and Fish aquarium exhibit.

2500+ attendees including 1500 school students.

One of the local and other schools environmental skits.

Arkansas Game and Fish Commission's project wild activities.

Grandpa Jones with his band providing entertainment.

Take Pride in America pin given to everyone.

Posters that were attached to trees in the exhibit area.

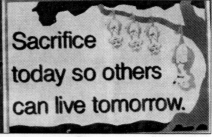

These signs are at the entrance of all parks.

Make Every Day Earth Day pin given to everyone.

Carl Garner's Affiliations and Awards

Affiliations

Registered Civil Engineer and Land Surveyor
Fellow in American Society of Civil Engineers (Lifetime member)
Former Regional Vice President of the National Water Safety Congress—25 years;
Served on Governor Pryor's Pick Up Arkansas Management Advisory Board;
Served on Governor Clinton's Resource Council;
Former Board Member Cleburne County Hospital Building Committee and Board of Directors;
Former member of Governor's Keep Arkansas Beautiful Commission;
Member of the Executive Board of Directors, Quapaw Area Council Boy Scouts of America (15 years);
Member of First Methodist Church, Heber Springs;
Board Member of Save Greers Ferry Lake, Inc.;
Member Lyon College Athletic Hall of Fame Selection Committee.

Awards:

Explorers, Boy Scouts of America William H. Spurgeon III Award
Service Master, National Association of Intercollegiate Athletics Distinguished Graduates.
Boy Scouts of America Silver Beaver Award Quapaw Council.
National Water Safety Congress National Appreciation Award
National Presidential Awards (3)
Lifetime Achievement Award (only one ever given).
National Society of the Daughters of the American Revolution National Conservation Award.
Greers Ferry Lake and Little Red River Association Distinguished Service Award, Silver Anniversary Award and Award of Honor, Arkansas Distinguished Senior Award
Congressional Record Senate National Tribute, Arkansas Senate Citation

State of Arkansas Certificate of Recognition,

Corps of Engineers Little Rock District Civilian of the Year Awards

Arkansas Federal Employee of the Year

Arkansas Parks and Tourism Department, Henry Award, Tourism Man of the Year Award and Hall of Fame Award

Arkansas Governor Clinton's Award of Excellence

Corps of Engineers Special Achievement Award for Planning and execution of Greers Ferry Dedication by President John F. Kennedy

Arkansas College (Lyon) Distinguished Alumnus Award, Athletic Hall of Fame and Honorary Doctorate Degree of Humane Letter honoris causa

Little Red River Audubon Society Earth Day Award

Department of the Army Decoration for Exceptional Civilian Services and Decoration for Meritorious Civilian Service. (Army's highest and 2nd highest awards for civilians)

Arkansas Able Distinguished Senior Employee Award

Keep America Beautiful 1st Iron Eyes Cody Award

The National Environmental Council National Environmental Achievement Award

Arkansas Game and Fish Foundation Hall of Fame Award

Sulphur Rock High School Distinguished Graduate Award

Baptist Health Amazing Spirit Award

Greers Ferry Lake and Little River Annual Cleanup Hall of Fame Award.

AWARDS

Employees of Greers Ferry Res Office and Little Rock office with Major Dad star Gerald McRainey and Linda Evans after receiving the project's Take Pride In America fifth First Place award and the Hall of Fame award.

Carl Garner receiving the Department of the Army Decoration of Exceptional Civilian Service Award from the Secretary of the Army in the Pentagon. This is the Army's highest civilian award.

Keep Arkansas Beautiful Foundation Outstanding Achievement Award.

Dr. John Zirsky, Acting Under Secretary of the Army presenting Garner with the US Flag flown over the Capitol.

Keep America Beautiful first Iron Eyes Cody award.

Baptist Health Amazing Spirit Award.

Governor Jim Guy Tucker presenting Garner with the Arkansas Senior Employee award.

Former Miss America Donna Axom and Miss Arkansas Heather Hunnicutt presenting Garner the Arkansas Parks and Tourism Hall of Fame award.

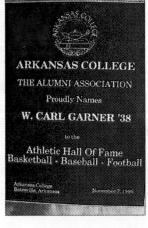

Arkansas College (Lyon) Athletic Hall of Fame Award – Basketball, Baseball, and Football.

The National Water Safety Congress Lifetime Achievement award.

THE PORTRAIT
OF PATTI UPTON

In the 70s and 80s the time era was still a man's world, and to get ahead you had to live by a man's code. Meeting Patti, she is very much a woman ... knows how to dress, and wear the right shade of lipstick. But there's more mystery to this woman than has been written about her.

Patti Upton gave birth to this powerful company called Aromatique literally "just for the fun it." She mixed together a jumble of botanicals that were native to her living in the Ozark Mountains. There were acorns, pinecones, gumballs, and hickory nuts available for the pleasure of gathering them. She fragranced them with spices, oils and imagination with how they affected her. Did their fragrance make her feel good, happy, comfortable or blah? No matter what, the mixture unknowingly at the time laid the cornerstone for Patti and her multimillion-dollar empire. That's how Aromatique, the company she founded in 1982 got its start. But it takes more than a good idea. Has this lady always been keen minded, shrewd, smart and foxy when it comes to the business end of her in money making, and working by a man's code?

Patti was born in Jonesboro in the northeastern corner of the state with a silver spoon in her mouth. She attended Stephens College, previously an all women's school in Missouri where she received the Christian Dior Award for her creativity. From Stephens, she finished at the University of Arkansas at Fayetteville. She represented the school as Miss University of Arkansas. While in Fayetteville, she met her husband, Richard (Dick) Upton. Patti grew up in a prosperous family and married into another one, so money was never a problem.

To add to this hodgepodge, here is a young woman, who had an excellent education, dressed well (which she claims is because of 'having a good eye') and spending some time in a weekend home on Greers Ferry Lake. This heightened Patti's sureness and a curiosity about nature. She also had three men behind her, the love of her life, husband Dick, who was an astute businessman in Memphis, and her twin sons. She and her family began to spend more time in this weekend home, and it eventually became home. Patti said, "Heber was a good place for the boys to grow up, but the hills can get lonely." Her mind was clear, and she had time for thinking and enjoying nature and meeting new friends. First she concentrated on being a good wife and mother, and in between time Patti found herself. It was time for this woman to have a personal time from the stream of parties and the life of the big city.

In the early 1980's Patti met Sandra Horne, who owned a well-known gift shop in Heber Springs called The Browsing Post'. Patti said, "She let me play and have a good time and fluff things up."

One day Horne said, "Why don't you do something new for the shop for the holidays?" And Patti did!

Patti's first creation was called *The Smell of Christmas*. Customers were bewitched. Much to Patti's surprise, it was an overnight miracle. This fragrance is now the company's flagship fragrance. It has been noted that it is great to create a wonderful fragrance, but to keep that fragrance at the top of the line for several years is amazing.

Patti is quick to call Aromatique a "we" company. She attributes Aromatique's success to the unique collection of people and talent on her staff who have been drawn to the breathtaking natural beauty of the company's home in Heber Springs, Arkansas, located in the Greers Ferry Lake resort area. The company employs over 400 local residents and is a boon to the local economy. With the establishment of Aromatique's flagship store, Panache, and the popularity of its ever-expanding line of products, the company has drawn many people from all over the nation and the world to Cleburne County.

Aromatique's commitment to generosity has helped several organizations throughout the years. The University of Arkansas for Medical Science, one of the top teaching hospitals in the United States, has been the recipient of nearly three-quarter of a million dollars. A few years ago Patti created a product called, *The Natural State*, which has helped raise money for the Nature Conservancy. Through the sale of these products, over 1.7 million dollars has been donated to the cause of preserving the natural environment for future generations to enjoy. The money has been used to help protect and preserve beautiful natural lands. Nancy DeLamar, Director of External Affairs for the South Central Division of The Nature Conservancy, said, "Through this unique and creative partnership which the success of Aromatique comes, many other organizations have benefited monetarily through the donation of products, time and services as well."

These charitable donations earned Patti Upton the Distinguished Citizen Award from local NBC affiliate KARK-TV and the Office of the Governor of the State of Arkansas.

Numerous magazines, newspapers and television shows have featured Patti and Aromatique. She appeared twice on *Working Woman,* a nationally syndicated television show from Washington, D.C. and *Lifestyles of the Rich and Famous* did a segment on Patti's Company. *The London Sunday Express* and *The Washington Post* newspapers have both traveled to Arkansas to interview Patti and focus on the company. A Christmas issue of *Victoria, a Hearst Magazine,* featured Patti and the Upton's Arkansas home. The following spring, *Victoria* and *Hearst* magazines invited her to the World Trade Center in New York City to speak on her creation of this successful decorative fragrance company. *Hearst Books* then included Patti and the Aromatique story in the publication of *The Business of Bliss.* An article in the November 2002 issue of *Southern Living* profiled the company and its varied products from decorative fragrance to the bath.

Creating only the highest quality products and keeping Aromatique at the forefront of the decorative fragrance industry has been the company's mission from the beginning. Patti Upton has been the driving force behind that mission. She states, "The quest for perfection is so important, it sometimes takes up to two years to develop a fragrance. We have always been known for the quality of our fragrances, and as we celebrate our 25th anniversary, our commitment to our customers remains strong and will not change. Aromatique will always provide the best products available and will continue to be the leader in the decorative fragrance industry."

Her colleagues in the business community have recognized Patti with numerous awards for her accomplishments. She has been named one of the top businesswomen in Arkansas by *Arkansas Business,* the state's top business weekly. Patti serves on the Board of Directors of AT&T Inc. She is a member of AT&T Corporate Public Policy and Environmental Affairs Committee and serves on the AT&T Human Resources Committee.

Patti and Dick have always been involved with the community and in charitable activities. Through Aromatique she finds she can do even more to give back some of the things which she has been blessed.

Patti's husband, Dick recently purchased a resort called The Red Apple Inn in an enchanting part of Arkansas called Eden Isle. This resort is only eight miles from Aromatique's headquarters. It was not solely a business decision, but rather an effort to preserve a historical site that had fallen upon bad times. Patti has put her creativity to work once again in the redecorating of the Inn. "It is our gift to the people of Arkansas," says Patti. And with a mystic look, she looks at Dick, and says, "and to ourselves."

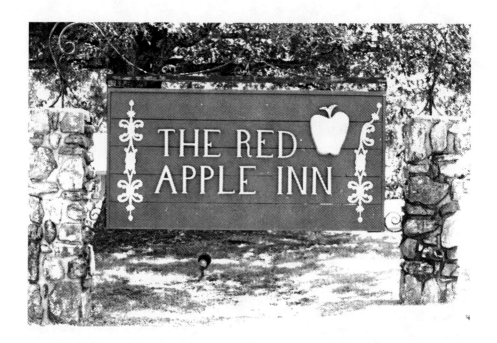

This still young woman has ridden 'the crazy merry go round of life'. It's been bumpy at times, but she is a woman 'who is able to roll with the punches'. But the most important thing that has happened to Patti in these Ozark Mountains is 'she found herself.' And the world found Patti Upton! She has made a big difference in the lives of many Arkansans and the nation through her big heart and giving back in many ways. She has created a business, a family, and a tradition of caring for others.

AWARDS:

Business & Professional Leader Award, Rotary International Paul Harris Fellowship award

Top 500 United States Business Woman—*Working Woman Magazine*

The Nature Conservancy Award for Outstanding Contribution to the Environment

Distinguished Citizen—KARK-TV and Office of the Governor of the State of Arkansas

The Women's Museum Advisory board

Corporations That Make a Difference—International Women's

Forum
Society of Entrepreneurs, Memphis, Tennessee
Citizen of the Year—Scottish Rite Masons of Arkansas
Pioneer Award-Arkansas Jaycees
Arkansan of the Year-Easter Seal Society
Director's Choice Award-National Women's economic Alliance
Outstanding Arkansas Corporation for Philanthropy
Arkansas Business Woman Owner of the Year
Arkansas Business of the Year
Arkansan of the Year-Arkansas Broadcasters' Association
National Pi Beta Phi Crest Award for Outstanding Alumnae
Arkansas Business Leadership in the 90's—Woman to Watch
Arkansas Professional Women of Distinction Award Winner

THE FALLING OF MILLER METEORITE IN 1930 IN GREERS FERRY, ARKANSAS

❖

Compliments of The Sun Times, written by Chastine Shumway

Julian and Pearl Bailey owned a farm on Highway 92 in the religious community of Miller now called Greers Ferry. Residents of that area will be more acquainted with the farm location now which Todd Davis owns across the street from F. L. Davis hardware store. The oak tree in the front yard is still standing where the meteorite rested for a short time. On this particular humid Sunday morning, the Bailey family was getting ready to attend the Post Oak Baptist Church services. Their large family had their usual breakfast of bacon, sausage, eggs, hot biscuits and chocolate gravy. Dressed in their Sunday best the family was about ready to go out the door and pick up kinfolk and neighbors on their way to church. Julian had the only mode of transportation in the area which w as a pickup truck. He had made sideboards and benches in the bed of the truck so everyone could be comfortable.

About 9:00 a.m. an earsplitting sound of roaring and popping filled the air. The house and ground vibrated. Little seven-year-old Leon Bailey said, "I think an airplane hit the ground."

Julian charged out of the door with his sons, Oather, Kenneth and Leon following. Swirls of smoke filled the air above a dry dirt roadbed next to his crop of waist high corn about 50 yards from their home. Julian hot-footed it over to the smoldering glowing object on the ground with just the tip of it showing. He did not know what it was.

Julian's brother John and his nephew Hobert were walking over to Julian's house to ride to church with them. Suddenly they heard and saw this heavenly body hurling to the earth from outer space. He said "The flight of this object racing through space looked like a white pigeon, but was moving much faster." Continuing he said, "When it landed it mush-roomed into a huge cloud of dust."

The hole it made in the ground was 18 inches in depth and was coated with a thin ebony crust. It was a stony meteorite, not a metallic one and shaped like a heart. The specimen was unique in that the margins of the under surface were radically grooved. These markings were developed while passing rapidly through the earth's atmosphere, implying that the specimen did not turn over while in transit.

Nothing was going to deter Julian, a staunch Baptist and Democrat from continuing his plans of attending church that Sunday morning. After they attended church services, they came home to a crowd of people from surrounding communities viewing the strange object. When it had cooled down some John was going to pick it up, but Julian said, "No, it may be contaminated or it might explode."

Finally after they saw that it was harmless, John dug it up and with the help of Julian's son Oather carried it to the big Oak tree in their front yard. Kenneth and Leon the younger sons cleared the path of the people who came far and wide to observe this marvel. People began chipping at the meteorite with their pocketknives getting pieces of it to take home. One man brought a hammer and began pounding on it. The rural postman offered to buy it for $20.00. The heart shaped meteorite weighed 36 pounds and 10 ounces. The local Headliner newspaper wanted to do a story on this occurrence. Julian got his nephew, Hobert Bailey out of school to tell about the falling. Hobert often told people, "I got out of school and Uncle Julian paid me."

Julian was an enterprising man. He hauled it to two fairs, charging people a small fee to see it, but that was more trouble than he anticipated, so back under the Oak tree it remained for some time. Realizing he had a diamond in the rough oddity, Julian took bids from various museums to sell the meteorite. Later Julian sold the meteorite for $800.00 to a J. P. Morgan, a wealthy businessman in New York. After he sold it, he said he had enough money to get a new car. It is believed that Julian purchased a new 1932 Plymouth car with the money.

November 11, 1930, "A New Meteorite" (the Miller Meteorite) through the generosity of Mr. J. P. Morgan was given to The American Museum of celestial immigrants for observation. The J. Lawrence Smith Fund of the National Academy of Sciences gave a grant toward the cost of investigating the Meteorite.

Julian and Pearl Bailey

THE DAVIS DYNASTY

✦

(An American Saga)

Todd and Adria Davis at farm on Hwy. 92. They are the beginning of the
Davis Dynasty.

The Davis family ... Pictured from left, Dana Leigh, Tammy Renae,
Rhonda Joyce, Debra Sue and Kristi Michelle. Sitting, Cleta and F.L.
Davis.

What does the word Dynasty mean? The dictionary definition of the word is a succession of rulers from the same family or line, and a family or group that maintains powers for several generations. Dynasty is a strong word for the Davis family of Greers Ferry, Arkansas, but it's true. Their achievements were and are the foundation of being part of the major building of the community of Stark, Arkansas, now Greers Ferry, Arkansas. The Davis family represents the American saga of Arkansas, romance, the can-do spirit, adventure, sweat and tears.

In the early 50's Faydlee's well-known father Todd Davis was the man about town. He was married to Adria Davis. They had three children, two sons, Faydlee and Billy Gene and one daughter, Uties. Todd owned large amounts of properties in the area. He was the owner of a sale barn and was an auctioneer for several sale barns. He farmed and had several head of cattle. If you needed anything, you called magnanimous Todd Davis. This author who knew the Davis' way back when gives credit, as others do to Todd Davis for his oldest son Faydlee Davis interests in business challenges. All through his life, like his father, he has enjoyed organizing, operating and assuming the risks for business ventures. In fact Todd told me that before my father, Richard Lohman, passed away that they were planning a catfish pond for the flowing spring on our property.

Faydlee graduated from the 8th grade and was the valedictorian of his class. The definition of valedictorian is a student usually of the highest scholastic standing and one who delivers the farewell oration at graduation. After graduating he gained most of his education from his father in working with him on their farm instead of attending high school. This was normal at that time. His father was above board with him, but he saw that Faydlee earned and worked for everything he got from him. His father gave him proceeds of his share of the cotton crop and Faydlee was so proud when he was able to buy his first truck and tractor with the money he had earned. But then one of the biggest challenges of his life was when he met a girl named Cleta Nored from Pleasant Ridge who showed up in the picture. This meeting was going to be a change in both of their lives, a metamorphous change, which would make them financially stable in the future. These two young country kids who never traveled out of Arkansas would eventually have the opportunity to visit 29 different countries, debt free. Shocked? Well this is America!

Let's travel back to the exciting time of this era beginning in the 1940's to the Stark community nestled in the Ozark Mountains. This was a little place of God loving people, which would eventually be called Greers Ferry when the Lake came in. This was a community that was closely knitted with their neighbors and relatives but would in course of time welcome newcomers who played a big part in the growth of the city to be of Greers

Ferry. In order to discuss the existence of this vicinity, let's meet some of the meaningful characters that played a major role in forming it.

Todd Davis moved his family from Edgemont, Arkansas to Stark, Arkansas and bought a farm with an old-fashioned farm house on several acres from Julian Bailey located on Highway 92. In the Pleasant Ridge community lived the Nored family who had three beautiful daughters and one son. Cleta Nored was the eldest daughter and attended West Side High School. She enjoyed going on the bus to the basketball games. At school while listening to the girls from Edgemont talk about their social life Cleta heard the name Faydlee mentioned quite often. She would think to herself, "If I never meet this Faydlee Davis it will be too soon." After one of the basketball games Faydlee asked her if he could take her home. She said, "Yes" and they made a date for the following Sunday night. Her father said she could go but to come straight home. They didn't get home soon enough and her father drove up in his Studebaker pickup truck and said, "Get in Cleta." After that incident she didn't expect to ever see Faydlee again, but he was determined to see her again. Later Faydlee told her he wanted to show her father that he would be back.

Meanwhile when Cleta graduated from West Side School, her Granny Nored gave her two cows and a calf. Cleta's father told her to go to the Arkansas National Bank and borrow money on the animals to be able to attend Draughans Business College. Cleta was frightened when she went to talk to the bank President, U.S. Hensley. Later on she realized that her father was preparing her for the business world by having her do this. She is now certain that President Hensley had heard from her father before she went in for the loan, but her father never would admit it. She then attended and graduated from Draughans College with a stenographic degree. After college she went to work for the Industrial Hygiene Division of the State of Arkansas. Faydlee and she corresponded by letter while Cleta was in Little Rock. On Thanksgiving weekend in 1952, Faydlee proposed. They were married March 22, 1953. They did not have a big wedding, as their family could not afford it. The minister arrived four hours late. The rains had flooded the Shiloh Bridge and the preacher had to ride a log truck in order to get to the wedding. After the wedding the newly-weds had to take him to Brownsville.

Faydlee continued to farm with his father. They planted crops of corn and cotton. As soon as they got the crops "laid by" Faydlee returned to Wilson Wholesale Grocery to drive the delivery truck, delivering groceries and feed. This was hard work. Feed only came in 100-pound bags and when they got feed in on a railroad car in Searcy, Faydlee would have to haul it at night.

In 1954 he decided to try to purchase a small grocery store and gas station (gas was 29 cents a gallon then) and thus have his own business. On November 11, 1954 his dream became a reality. They went to the Cleburne County Bank and borrowed $500.00 to complete this transaction. Faydlee, Cleta and their new baby Rhonda moved into the living quarters of the Miller grocery and assumed ownership November 11, 1954.

Faydlee and his father-in-law decided to work together and had rented some land in the Miller bottoms, which is now under water. Faydlee thought it would be good for him to continue farming while Cleta operated the store. In the winter he would also be available to help with the grocery. He spent many of his nights hauling feed for the store from Little Rock.

A few years later the government began to buy land for the Greers Ferry Lake. Faydlee realized he would have to move his family because Miller was to be in the heart of the lake. F.L. as he was now called, began to look at other areas. They took a trip into Oklahoma and into North Arkansas but when his dad offered to give him 20 acres in the Stark community he decided this might be best. On February 29, 1960 they made the move to Stark and opened up their new store, F. L. Davis Mercantile. He began employing family members and trusted friends to help with this venture. They had their *Grand Opening* March 12, 1960.

Pearl and Daulton, Cleta's parents helped in the store, and later when they built a Western store, F.L.'s mom worked there and Todd hauled feed for them from Little Rock. The ladies made sandwiches in the back of the store for the family and anyone else who might drop in and buy one.

Every penny counted! F.L. and Cleta sold their grocery inventory in 1972, thus ending their work in the grocery business. There was a need for Cleta to help F.L.

In the early 60's the area saw the need for telephones and banks. A group of citizens met, and Cleta was appointed to head the telephone committee. She and the committee worked diligently with Southwestern Bell and before long SWB took over the tedious work.

Several of the businessmen began to talk of incorporating a city. In order to get a bank, there would have to be an incorporated city with at least 200 people. The committee decided to go with the name of Greers Ferry capitalizing on the expected popularity of Greers Ferry Lake. A mayor and other officials were needed. There was no doubt in anyone's mind who the first mayor would be. That was the job for F.L. Davis. He was elected as the first mayor of Greers Ferry. He also served as a member of the West Side School Board.

In the mid 60's F.L. bought his first 18-wheeler and cattle trailer. He used it at night to haul cattle from Ash Flat or Batesville to Fort Smith. Sometimes after hauling a load of cattle to Fort Smith he would wash out the trailer and go on to Arkansas City, Kansas to bring back a load of wheat bran and shorts (hog feed). The wheat bran and shorts were in 100-pound bags. These days were long and tiresome!

Some years later he began to haul cattle from Pine Bluff and Eagle Mills, Arkansas to different feed lots out west. At one time he had six trucks on the road. Cleta made the truck reports and sometimes went to Eagle Mills to run down a truck driver to get the paperwork. Sonny Majors, one of the first truck drivers, hauled his first load of cattle in 1968.

When the Greers Ferry Lake began to fill, and people began to come and purchase property, F.L. saw the need for a builder's supply. He had carried many items such as plumbing and electrical supplies in the grocery store but that was not enough. One day a man from Cave City came in and said that he wanted to buy a house pattern. F.L. explained to him that he did not have lumber. He assured him that he would see if he could find a place to buy it. After several phone calls he gave the man a price and he bought it immediately. Fred James had come to work for F.L. by this time and he hauled the first load of lumber in a cattle trailer. The sale gave F.L. the fever. After this little venture F.L. had the foresight to see that there would be a great need for a lumberyard with all the building expected in and around the Lake. When Greers Ferry Lake came in many newcomers were interested in moving to this beautiful area. Real-estate sales hit the highest peak that had ever been seen. Fred James was F.L.'s right hand man in this venture. He worked for him until his death in October 2006. Another loyal employee who still works with the Davis' business is Wilma Hartsfield. She has worked for the Davis family since November of 1967. This was the beginning for the Davis' and the community in the booming lumber and building supply business. He added a couple of flatbed trailers and hauled all his lumber, plywood, and roofing for the store. It would not be too many years until F.L. would venture out again. Several men came from Stuttgart who were carpenters. They built many homes and buildings in this area, but went back to Stuttgart intermittently to continue their work there. Yet, they continued to buy their supplies from F.L. They encouraged him to come to Stuttgart and put in a lumber business. In 1975 he bought out an old Oyster Bar and turned it into a builder's supply business. John Morton, a reputable young man who was born and raised in the area moved there and operated the store for him. John was only 19 years old and many people said it would never work. But with his eagerness to help and F.L.'s ingenuity it worked! F.L. later built a new store and opened the first Do-It Center in the State of Arkansas in Stuttgart.

Some years later, F.L. took a sabbatical from the lumberyard in the middle 70's and drove one of the trucks himself for about 5 years. Cleta drove with him off and on for approximately 3 years. They did what they had to do to keep the bills paid!

In between all of this work, he and Cleta were having children, all girls who became an important asset in their lives and businesses. Petite Cleta had an outgoing personality and stood by her man in all his endeavors. In between filling in wherever she was needed, she sometimes drove a truck. Cleta has always been active in school and church. She has served as a leader in Bible Study Fellowship in Conway since 1982. Throughout the years their five daughters won in several beauty and talent contests. Cleta was an excellent mother, and even today, the girls all live close by and are a loving and warm family.

As their daughters were growing up, F.L. did not advertise much. It seemed that word of mouth was the best advertisement for them. In the early 80's he and Cleta decided that 'all work and no play' was getting to be a habit. They came up with an idea to have annual fish fries for their customers and friends in appreciation for helping the Davis' in being successful with their businesses. In the beginning this was lots of fun for the people and the girls. Excitement filled the air, as employees were busy in getting the lumberyard cleaned up. Different companies came and helped fry fish. The crowd would arrive at 4:00 p.m., and by 6:00 p.m. there wasn't a place to park. The menu consisted of fried fish, French fries, slaw, hush puppies and sliced onions. Many ladies brought desserts. Local bands played music. There was clogging and the Davis girls and Cleta would sing. Around 500 people came every year. The Davis' were a fun family and this annual affair was greatly appreciated by everyone.

Cleta and F.L. didn't have much personal time with their busy lives. Cleta remembers a time when they were first married that Todd gave them a very appreciative gift. It was $5.00 to go to the movies. This was one of the most memorable times in their busy lives. She said there were times when they didn't know where their next penny would come from. Most of the money which was made was turned back into the many endeavors F.L. had jumped into quickly. He was always looking for something else to help provide for his large family. Six women in his life were very costly. He remembers while trying to buy a liftfork, he ended up buying a store in Morrilton. Renae, their second daughter and her husband took it over and ran it for several years before selling it.

In 1995 F.L. decided to spread his wings a little further. He bought a piece of land where there had previously been a store from the Shannon's in Clinton. Their building had burned and they did not intend to build back. F.L. began building there and the store was completed and opened in November of 1995 with daughter Rhonda Joyce as the manager. After a few years Brent Hunt, the oldest grandson came on board.

F.L. associated himself with many fine reputable companies. One of those companies gave him a nice incentive. If he excelled in buying more of their products from the company every year he would win trips to travel throughout the world. This was a goal to which F.L. looked forward to as he and Cleta enjoyed traveling together.

In 2002, Governor Mike Huckabee honored F.L. as being an "Outstanding Citizen of the State of Arkansas." F.L. is a member of the Cleburne County Economic Development Commission and the advisory board of the First Arkansas Bank and Trust.

In 2000 another store was built in Heber Springs. It was a unique store, different from the rest of the Davis' stores. It boasted a large gift center section and has 22,500 square feet of floor space. Renae Baker is the owner of this store. The girls are now grown and have major positions in the Davis Dynasty. Their grandchildren are active in keeping the Davis Dynasty reputation alive. F.L. wants the Davis' stores to always remain a family affair. A daughter Debra, a grandson Jayce, a granddaughter Brandy and her husband Lee all work in the Greers Ferry store. Dana makes payroll for the Heber Springs store as well as teaching in Heber springs High School, ASU Heber Springs and works for the Corps of Engineers from spring to fall. Kristi works for Midstate Medical Supply in Conway, Arkansas.

The Davis family is generous in their support of worthwhile projects for Cleburne County, but most of their support goes to churches and schools. Although F.L. Davis has a quiet relaxed unexcitable manner, the Davis' live their lives with a rare earnestness. F.L. achieved more than he had ever dreamed of by pursuing his ambitions with never a negative thought. Throughout all of this public esteem, F.L. and his family have remained unchanged. They still live in the same pleasurable brick home across from his father's home. Their door is always opened to all, and in his quiet, cool headed way he is without arrogance and is a friend to all.

F.L. and Cleta say they owe their success to God and the closeness and hard work of their family and friends. It will be interesting to see what else is in store for the Davis family and their addendum to their American Saga in the future for their treasured land of Arkansas.

STATE OF ARKANSAS

To All Who Shall See These Presents, Greeting:

Know Ye, that I, the Governor of the State of Arkansas, in the name and by the authority of the people of this State, as vested in me by the Constitution and Laws of the State of Arkansas, reposing special recognition for the distinguished accomplishments, services and deeds of the Citizens of Arkansas, do hereby award to:

F. L. Davis

this

CERTIFICATE OF APPRECIATION

as an outstanding Citizen of the State of Arkansas, having shown to the people of Arkansas an outstanding interest in public service to this State. In Testimony Whereof, I have hereunto set my hand this 22nd day of February in the Year of Our Lord, Two Thousand and two.

Mike Huckabee
Governor

This certificate of appreciation was bestowed on F.L. Davis by Mike Huckabee for being an outstanding citizen of the state of Arkansas.

Cleta stands in front of F.L. and Cleta Davis' first business in Miller.

CHILDHOOD MEMORIES OF THE OZARKS
By Cleta Davis

When I was but a little girl
In the hills of Arkansas,
I watched the sun set through the trees
As I sat on my favorite log.

This log holds many memories
'Twas there I went to play
With cousin Betty and our dolls
We went nearly every day!

We've sewn many lovely shirts and hats
With pine needles and hickory leaves.
Made high heeled shoes from empty spools
We were never hard to please.

We had no radios or CD players
No television, computers and such.
We made our own entertainment
For us it didn't take much.

We cut out paper dolls and clothes
From the Sears Roebuck catalogue,
Made whistles out of hickory limbs
And blew them all day long.

We walked around on homemade stilts
Our fathers had made for us.
It took a while for us to learn
But we would learn or bust!

Rainy days were spent inside
There were homemade games to play.
We played fox and geese on a homemade board
Pop made for us one day.

We made fudge and Molasses candy,
No mixes, we made them from scratch
We loved to learn from Granny
As a teacher, there was no match.

Winter came and our first snow
Was such an awesome sight!
We could hardly wait to get outside
Where we played 'till almost night.

Our parents called us for supper
Then there was our homework to do.
A bath, then snuggled in feather beds
We slept the whole night through!

'Twas morning! I heard the rooster crow
As I scampered out of bed.
Another school day will soon begin
I must get my lesson read.

The time goes quickly ticking by
Then off to school we go.
To that little old two room school house
Just a few miles up the road.

No bus, no car, no pickup truck
We walked to school everyday.

Our group grew larger and larger
As we walked along the way.

There was Fayotta, then me, then Betty
As we meandered on our way.
Eulon, Ethan and Texelda joined us
Just the same routine everyday.

Next was Lavetta, Eva Dean and Cloeta
Maybe Gereta and Elfreeda too.
At the top of the hill Jean and Jerry
Just waiting, as little kids do.

By the time we got to the schoolhouse
We had accumulated quite a bunch.
"Books" took up, we studied hard
Just waiting for our "little red bucket" lunch.

No matter what the weather,
We walked everyday to school.
We learned "reading, writing and arithmetic"
Even memorized the Golden Rule.

We were rather quite a rowdy bunch
We could give the teacher lots of trouble.
But standing in a comer with our nose in a ring
Would burst any smart alecks bubble.

Sundays were about the same each week,
Spent in worship and songs of praise.
We learned from the Holy Bible
How the Father had ordered our days.

I was an only child for some nine years
Then along came a baby sister.
Little did I know my life would change
From the only one to a babysitter.

Well, a few years passed and guess what happened?
A brother arrived on the scene.
Then in a year and a half another surprise
A curly haired sister with eyes of green.

Well, time goes swiftly passing by,
The years, Oh! Where have they gone?
My childhood years, they all have passed
And now I'm almost grown.

Just look! I'm a high school senior?
Sixteen years of my life have gone by!
I'm standing on adulthood's threshold
Holding my diploma, with tears in my eyes.

God has so wonderfully blessed me!
With Christian parents and a lifetime of love.
I'm grateful for all they have given
Provided by the Heavenly Father above.

He gave to me life everlasting.
He is my guide 'long life's rugged way.
He gives me a hope for tomorrow,
Joy, peace and comfort today!

Cleta Davis' family ... seated, Pearl Mae, Cleta Joyce and John Daulton.
Standing, Rosetta Jean, Billy Joe and Rhonda Gail.

TORNADO TOPPLES EDGEMONT ARKANSAS BRIDGE

All that was left of the 1,377 foot long Edgemont Bridge that connected the communities of Edgemont, Greers Ferry, Fairfield Bay, Arkansas was nine piers which held up the superstructure after a devastating tornado twisted the steel and concrete bed off the piers March 15, 1984. It was estimated that the wind range was 450 miles per hour. A Greers Ferry woman was killed by the tornado.

Federal and state government officials wasted no time in this disaster and quickly helped alleviate some of the major problems this had caused in these areas.

One of the biggest problems with the destruction of the bridge was transportation across the lake. A ferry was eventually hired to solve this problem. Congressman Bill Alexander called a meeting of several state and federal officials immediately to determine the feasibility of a pontoon bridge or ferry system as temporary relief for transportation across the lake.

The twister destroyed the Greers Ferry Water Treatment Plant. In addition, the system served Edgemont and Fairfield Bay. Estimated damage of the system and contents was $250,000. Approximately 160 drums were provided by the United State Air Force.

Halbert Guyot of the First Electric Cooperative described the destruction to power lines as the worst in the history of Cleburne County. Crews from other parts of the state joined local workers to restore electricity before the conclusion of the weekend. The feeder line broke along state Highway 92 and caused the outage. By rerouting the power areas electricity was received at different times. Over 400 customers lost telephone service because of the storm.

Governor Clinton visited the area and declared that a state of disaster emergency existed in the area. He established the sum of $50,000 of state money to be used by the state Office of Emergency Services to provide supplemental disaster relief, primarily individual assistance to disaster victims.

Representative Ed Bethune cited the economic tragedy involved. He said, "The loss of the bridge was like cutting the economic lifeline."

THE PORTRAIT OF ARTIST GLYNDA TURLEY

Glynda believes God gives everyone talents, and sometimes the talents are different. She says, "The choice to use and develop that talent is ours. It is a gift and responsibility that I don't take lightly. God expects us to do our part. He will open doors and opportunities if we will walk through. I hope others will be encouraged and inspired to seek their dreams by knowing my story. I don't want to be remembered for selling a lot of paintings. I want to be remembered for the difference my paintings have made in someone else's life."

Glynda LaVonne Deckard was born in 1947 in Heber Springs, Arkansas. She grew up in the small rural community of Ida, Arkansas. She was the only daughter of Voyd and Wincel Deckard. Glynda attended Wilburn School in Cleburne County.

Glynda spent many days with her grandmother, Bertha Liles, who was the light of her childhood. They made crafts and tended flowers together.

Glynda says, "Our porch swing overlooked my grandmother's flower garden. The swing was one of my favorite places to daydream. I spent hours in it studying the petals on my grandmother's roses and hollyhocks. Sometimes I would lie on my back in the grass and study the white clouds floating overhead that resembled different shapes which stirred up my imagination." The nostalgia for the past shows in some of her exceptional pictures, which usually tell a story.

Although she grew up on a small farm with animals, she never had time for pets. She was more interested in drawing pictures of them than playing with them. In later life she painted pictures of farm scenes with mules, horses, chickens and sheep.

As a child Glynda sketched pictures in church and in school. She often sketched pictures of her classmates. Her parents scolded her for wasting her school paper. Therefore, she learned to be thrifty and never let paper go to waste. No one thought she would become famous, so her talent was not encouraged. Glynda had no hope of becoming a successful and famous artist as she is now. This seemed out of reach, because art was not offered in the schools, and art supplies could not be bought locally. She did not have a role model artist to look up to, but a strong urge compelled her to keep working at a talent she loved. She continued to do black and white pencil sketches which would eventually pay off for her. She also enjoyed browsing through the Sears Catalog and cutting out paper dolls and sketching clothes for them. She did not realize that this was in God's plan, and someday her framed artwork would be in several catalogs in the future.

She said, "My grandmother, who was a great seamstress, would not have dreamed that someday there would be fabrics with my designs on them which would be made into bedding and bath products, tiffany lamps and outdoor flags, and other items for major companies such as J.C. Penny.

Glynda married her teenage sweetheart. Jerry Turley in 1964. He encouraged her in fulfilling her dream. Glynda began painting in the medium of oils. She produced meticulous works containing many of the designs that enhanced an ever-increasing display of licensed products. She drew much inspiration from the beauty of pastoral scenes in the country-side and the Ozark Mountains.

As a young wife and mother of two small children, a neighbor asked her about giving her children drawing and painting lessons. She had never considered teaching, but this began her art career and a much-needed income to buy art supplies that were now more available. She began teaching from her kitchen table. For every two dollars she received for a lesson taught, she ordered an art instruction book through the mail. Demand for art lessons took her from her kitchen table to night classes at a friend's small beauty shop in Pangburn. This led to teaching private art lessons to groups of children on the campus of Pangburn School in neighboring White County. She also taught art classes throughout Arkansas in different arts and craft stores. This led to buying a partnership in a Heber Springs craft business. During her thirteen years of teaching she taught children from five years of age to senior adults in their eighties. Glynda attributes those special years of teaching to her growth as an artist. She says with a chuckle, "I think I learned more than they did." After a student made a slip of the brush on her painting and felt it could not be corrected, Glynda took her brush and demonstrated how easy it was to change it. One art student called Glynda's brush, 'The Magic Brush.'

Glynda gives God the credit for her natural gift of artistry and her good fortune. She had no formal art training at all. She says, "I have learned by trial and error, and I am still learning." She has painted several scenes of country churches. She said, "The church is a gratifying foundation for Arkansas families. Churches play a large part in all of the God fearing Arkansan's lives from childhood to adulthood, to death." The churches Glynda paints radiates the history of the hill people of Arkansas.

Sunday on Cades Cove, the second in a series of paintings by Glynda Turley. Glynda is an example of why the people are so special in my book. She was thrilled because she was in the book, and I was blessed because she was one of the Unforgettables to allow me to do her story!

In the 1980's Glynda won top awards in the Governor's Exhibition and the Distinguished Artist Exhibition. Later she and her company would win runner up in the Arkansas Small Business of the year, only to be outdone by a trucking company. The most meaningful and favorite award is the award she received from ASU Beebe for the Outstanding Alumna for 2004.

Success as a professional artist went far beyond what she or her husband had imagined. The demand for Glynda's work from art galleries, furniture stores, and gift shops mushroomed overnight. Out of necessity, she had to give up teaching. Representatives from large gift companies tracked

Glynda and her art down at retail arts and crafts shows around the region. She hired them to sell her framed pictures to stores all over the United States. Later her work was shipped to stores in Canada, Australia, Japan, South Africa and other foreign countries. Orders came in so fast that she had to hire additional employees to cut mats and help frame the pictures. Glynda's husband gave up his construction business, and he and their son Shon began building frames. Glynda taught herself the art of mat cutting. Their daughter Shannon graduated college just at the right time with a degree in business management. Now she was ahead of that department. A few years later their son-in-law Rick and daughter-in-law Toni joined the company. Nieces, nephews, former students and friends were needed to be a part of Glynda Turley Prints, Inc. It was a family affair.

In 1992 a fire destroyed their five-year-old factory building. All of their manufacturing supplies, and Glynda's prints, as well as 96 original oil paintings were destroyed. But providence was with them. The faith and spirit of Glynda and her team saw it through. They received prayers from the local and people and fans from all over the world. God helped them to rebuild and grow that same year despite the fire. The growth in the company was so fast that soon over 150 employees were needed to keep up with the demand. Large manufacturing companies began licensing Glynda's designs for their products from Tiffany lamps, throws, pillows, Bible covers, calendars, greeting cards and much more. When the call came from New York to meet with the bedding manufacture, Glynda couldn't believe it.

The highlight of Glynda's career has been the sole artist to decorate and sell her work for five years at the Grand Palace in Branson, Missouri. Glynda Turley's art galleries and gift stores are in Branson, Missouri and Heber Springs, Arkansas as well as Gatlinburg, Tennessee. This affords her the opportunity to meet thousands of her collectors from all over the country. Having the opportunity to see the beautiful country we live in as she travels with her business is a big bonus as well. In 1994 she traveled to England and France on a business and pleasure trip.

She is proud that she has immortalized her grandchildren in her paintings, which is every grandmother's dream. Glynda strives to be a good ambassador for the State of Arkansas and Cleburne County. In her 25 plus years of traveling the country doing trade shows and personal appearances she is proud to let the world know where she was born and still lives.

She continues to paint many Arkansas scenes and landmarks. Several of her paintings are of the Old Mill in North Little Rock. Although the mill was used in the credits section of the movie 'Gone With the Wind' Glynda is quick to let the viewer know the mill is not in Georgia. Her 'Summer Stroll' painting portrays the Villa Marre, a historical home in Little Rock. It was the home in the popular television series. Designing Women. Glynda makes sure everyone knows Arkansas claims fame to these landmarks. She has also painted her husband, son-in-law and grandsons fishing the Little Red River with Sugar Loaf Mountain in the background, and it is appropriately named Little Red River. Glynda's company has donated hundreds of pieces of her artwork for special causes such as Relay for Life, Hospice as well as other Cancer and Health related drives, terminally ill patients. Special Olympics, St. Judes Hospital and many other children and school related causes.

Glynda Turley has certainly made a difference in Arkansas and the nation and will go down in history as one of the most noted women artists of her day, the future and the past. Her pictures have a freshness and spontaneity that will endure forever.

REX HARRAL, THE
WALKING HISTORY BOOK

Sitting under a large Willow Oak tree at Rex Harral's home in Wilburn, Arkansas was quite an experience. This man bewitched this author. Rex Harral is a blend of the mannerisms that make Arkansas a noteworthy state and America a great nation. Rex Harral has a deep love for God, his friends, and his community of Wilburn, Arkansas. He is a walking history book.

His family was one of the first settlers in the community of Old Corinth, which would eventually be called Wilburn, Arkansas.

This man instigated the forming of The Cleburne Historical Society, serving as President for many years. He has been a teacher at Wilburn School and is loved by the whole community. Time passed quickly, as Harral is a great teller *of true happenings of his life in his beloved Wilburn. Rex said in his Arkansas twang, "Nobody ever went hungry during the Depression or hard times in Wilburn. The people shared with each other. Helpful and meaningful neighborliness helped people survive the Depression. If anyone goes through hard times, I reckon this is the best place to be."*

I enjoyed hearing this man's down home wisdom. As long as we have people like Rex Harral with an imbedded strong American pioneer spirit, the history of our great land of America will never be lost. This man not only has made a difference in his community and state, but also has been elevated to the status of a 'National Gem'.

Stories of his fine craftsmanship has appeared in various magazines, including the National Geographic magazine and newspapers which bring worldwide travelers to his door to meet the man and purchase some of his unique crafts. The following is his story of growing up in Wilburn. The author has permission and has collaborated with Rex on writing some of his true tales in her book also. When Rex was five his mother sent Rex to school with his older brother the first day. The teacher gave a boy who was misbehaving a good shaking. Rex was so terrified, he hid under a bench. After that he did not return to school until he was six years old.

Rex Harral is an 87-year of age man of vintage who is an extraordinary jack of many trades. He was born in 1919 and raised in Wilburn, Arkansas. He lives on 110 acres he bought back in 1994. This farm is only two miles from where he was born. He has built everything that stands on this property. "He says, "There was nothing here. I built everything you see." He was referring to the house, the barn, two sheds and his beloved woodshed. His shop is very unique because he has a blacksmith kiln in it which he forged himself. In the middle of the shed is a large stove upon which is perched a hefty aluminum vat style pot. He soaks various splint strips of wood specimens, which he uses to repair cane-bottomed chairs and antique tables. He is known nationwide for his handcrafted cedar chests.

His father was an artist with a chopping ax and was an expert at hewing. His paternal grandfather was a carpenter and made chairs and furniture. His maternal great-grandfather was a blacksmith and could make a complete wagon, and he settled in Wilburn right after the Civil War. Wilburn was then called Old Corinth. The name was changed to Wilburn in 1903 when the town got a post office. At that time the Wilburn community raised cotton, corn and hay. Most farmers also had beef, cattle and milk cows, and some raised strawberries. Rex remembers that his father bought two or three barrels of flour at a time storing them in the smokehouse. The bags of flour were hanging from the ceiling so mice couldn't get in them. He also bought 100 pounds of sugar at a time. The coffee beans came in a tow sack and each family had a coffee grinder. When flour and feed sacks came about, they were valued as material for clothing. Rex was orphaned at age nine and along with several siblings was raised by his older sister, Letta Harral who was a teacher at Wilburn School.

At the age of 11, Rex made his first knife which he still has displayed in his home. This was the beginning of a diversified career of a craftsman. Today Rex is also nationally known as a toolmaker. Rex had little formal education but was street smart, and although poor, did not realize it. Even as a child he was born with an unusual capability to understand people, their thoughts, motives, and desires.

Rex is a renowned writer and storyteller who holds an audience spellbound and is much in demand to speak at schools, clubs, etc. One of his fondest memories was when he was asked to give the final speech to the last graduating program of the historical Wilburn High School, which was closed in 2006. The school held many memories for everyone, and this was a heart-felt time for the community of Wilburn. To this day, Rex can not speak of that moment without tearing up. For twenty years he taught seventh graders in Wilburn School how to carve.

Rex served in the Civilian Conservation Corps (CCC) as a leader in the 1930's where he was able to learn to use more sophisticated tools which were not available to him previously. After service he settled on a farm within two miles of his birthplace in Wilburn. His work shed shows antique tools that he still works with as well as modern tools. This rustic unpolished shop has been his paradise for 78 years. "If you want to make me mad," Rex Says, "Say something bad about my shop." Rex puts in 6 days at his shop.

Rex is an innovator as well as a creator. He says, "Very often, if I'm making something and need a tool, I will stop and make me one."

Mr. Harral makes all of his wooden crafts from trees on his farm in his treasured shop. He cuts and dries wood from hickory, persimmon, and oak and sassafras trees for his handcrafted bowls and vases. Rex is known for his unique berry picking buckets made from live bark when the sap is flowing. This piece shows his Native American heritage. His wooden churns command a price of $125.00. To this day, Rex makes his own country butter. Among other items are candlesticks, bowls, vases, ducks, and cedar chests, cane bottom chairs and pole beds. In 2004 he won "Best of Show at the Cleburne County Fair for his own design of candlesticks made from horseshoes. Rex is nationally known as a toolmaker. Rex says, "I'm the last of the old school blacksmiths in Arkansas." Every year he takes his portable forge to the Ozark Folk Center in Mountain View, Arkansas. He makes knife blades, horseshoes and dog collars. His hand-forged tools are much in demand. Rex also shows his work annually at the historic Arkansas Museum. "I exhibit my wares at an annual day of competition and demonstration by some of the best regional blacksmiths. Primarily, I make square nails for the kids and heat steel cable in my forge and make it into different sized hole punches. My hand forged tools always sell out before the day is over."

He also built the log house on display for the Garner's Visitor Center in Heber Springs, Arkansas.

Inside his old-timey cozy home is a room where he displays some of his blue-ribbon woodcrafts. One unusual item is a wooden shelf made out of hickory and cedar wood with a carved squirrel on it. On the bottom of this shelf are hand forged horseshoes made by him also attached to hang your coats on. He won first place with this unrivaled item. Another originality item is the "hillbilly diamond" that is carved from cedar. Among his collection is a chunk of wood depicting a walnut growing inside a tree. He has been offered $1,000 for this rare piece, but God's work of nature is too priceless to Rex to part with.

As a charter member of the Cleburne County Historical Society, Mr. Harral was instrumental in forming the organization. He was on the board of directors for many years and served several terms as President of the society. He has written articles on the *Life and Times of the Early Settlers of the Arkansas Ozarks*, and the history of Cleburne County that has been published in *The Sun Times, the CCHS Journal, The Ozarks Mountaineer* magazine and other publications. Mr. Harral also assisted on the research history of Cleburne County for the book, *'Time and the River'* and his picture is on the back of the book with the author Evalena Berry. Rex spins tales of pioneer life in the Ozark foothills. Rex authored one of the most popular books at the Historical Museum in Heber Springs called, *'Thanks for Listening'*.

Wilburn Basketball Team of 1930 ... Wilburn School basketball team won the county championship in 1930. Front row from left: Ollie Latch, Harvey Hazelwood, Carnell Jackson and Ed Shook. Back row from left: Garland Thomas, Sherwood Small, Adrain Tarver, Principal and Coach Oather Payton and Claud Altom.

REX HARRAL REMEMBERS
(Told to author, Chastine Shumway)

As I interviewed Rex many times under the big Willow Oak tree with his Australian dog, Floppie lying contentedly at Rex's feet, the present time escaped us. The time machine took us back to earlier days about his life and the history of Wilburn. We laughed and sometimes Rex teared up. Some of his stories the author has written has been the way Rex told his story to me. He was definitely the storyteller, speaking in first person. Although I am the author of The Unforgettables, I decided to write Rex' story as he was speaking in his Arkansas Twang. The author collaborated with Rex on writing these memorable 'once in a lifetime' stories'.

My name is Rex Harral. I was born in 1919 and raised in the community of Wilburn, Arkansas. My ancestors settled in this area before the Civil War. My mother was Mr. and Mrs. James Leonard and Ida Johnson. My education started in a 2-room school in 1925 on what is now called Tyler Road. Opal Cranford taught the first through fourth grades. Jarred Barker taught the fifth grade through the eighth grade. My second teacher Letta Harral taught the first grade through the fourth, and Floyd Ward taught the fifth grade through the eighth. In 1927 Center Chapel School consolidated with Wilburn. Their one room school was torn down and a 'T' shaped addition was added to Wilburn School. Adrian Tarver was principal. Letta Harral, my sister taught the first to third grade. Bertha Magness taught the 4th grade to the sixth, and Adrian taught seventh to tenth grades.

In 1928, Hiram consolidated with Wilburn. Ellis Ramsey built a wooden box on back of his lumber truck and hauled about 30 students from Hiram to Wilburn. This served as the first school bus. Adrian Tarver, Letta Harral, Audrey Shook and Kissinger Nowell were employed as teachers. A curtain was installed to separate some classrooms. December 1930 we were dismissed for Christmas at the four-room school. We went back to school January 1931. We had a new 5 class room school with an auditorium in a beautiful red brick building. Everyone was very proud that this was one of the most modem rural schools in Arkansas. Kitty Shook was the fifth grade teacher the remainder of that term. We were having split terms in those days, about 2 months in July through September and August and then dismissed for about 2 months for cotton picking. We went back to school in late October. At that time Adrian Tarver was principal.

Eve Cunningham and Eugene Cullum were the high school teachers. The twelfth grade was taught beginning that year with Letta Harral and Audrey Shook who were primary teachers. No twelfth grade diplomas were issued due to the school closing and the lack of money and insufficient credits and other problems at that time.

Wilburn School was first located on the Terry Plantation, sometimes referred to as Terry Springs. Records indicate it was in operation before the Civil War. The school was in a log cabin with a dirt floor, one window, one door and a fireplace at one end. For seating, split logs were used in the building, which had been used before for slaves on the Terry plantation. At that time the community was called "Old Corinth". It was not called Wilburn until 1903. This was located on what is now Center Ridge Road, about one mile south of intersection of Tyler Road. There is a spring still on Center Ridge road today that supplied water for the cabin. The late John Wilson (1870–1950) gave this information to me. He was a first grader on the first day of school there. The late Harvey Hazelwood, who was the nephew to of John Wilson and I went to John's home on now Dry Mountain Road to the first house north of Wilburn Creek. In 1947 his mind was very clear as he rattled off this information without hesitation.

The story of Wilburn School is quite a long story. Some of the information pertaining to Wilburn School has not been correct. According to my information I am not sure how many terms' school was held in that first cabin, but I think it was just one year. Next west to the log cabin church on Old Liberty Creek, there was a baptizing hole where many a person was baptized. The last time I was there the hole wasn't much more than knee deep. The building burned down and the school was then held in old Dr. Tucker's store building. A new building was later constructed at the north end of present Hazelwood farm on Dry Mountain Road. At that time the largest part of population was living north of the present day Wilburn. This new building was convenient for school kids. There is some confusion about the happenings of that building. Some say it was torn down and moved to now Tyler Road. My mother went to school there in 1898, and so did Ella Webster Robertson. Ella told me the building was typical box and batten, 1 x 12" yellow pine rough sawn nailed upright and battens over the cracks. When they left that building it was sold to an individual and was torn down and erected as a residence. The building on Tyler Road was made of planed lumber, known as drop siding and painted. The late Sherman Latch and Oscar Chandler said when they quit the school on now Dry Mountain Road, the school was held in the now General Baptist Church. Sherman was born in 1906 and started to school in the church on the first 1912 term in that church. The 2-story building had a lodge hall in the upper part.

I well remember that building. The building was renovated and the upper story was tom off in 1926–1927. School was held there for two terms, and a one-room school building was built on Tyler Road. The first term of school was held there in 1914. The second room was added in 1918. My own memory tells me that Center Chapel School consolidated with Wilburn in 1926 or 1927. My father helped Wyatt Roberson add the third room after the Center Chapel building was tom down and reconstructed. I remember my dad brought home some scrap lumber that was painted white and blue.

I was a board member in 1948 when the first school annual was published. The late Harvey Hazelwood was principal, and he asked me to go with him to interview his uncle, the late John Wilson, 1872–1949. Harvey or I did not take notes. The annual says the first school was 1880. I think John said 1878, so it is published in 1880, so we accept 1880 as the official date. I think he said one term was taught and then to Liberty House Church for several years. I recall very clearly that John said someone got mad and burned the church. It was then that they went to Dr. Tucker's old vacant store building, and then the school building at north end of now Hazelwood farm was built in 1889. School was held there most likely until 1912, and previously stated they started school in the now Baptist Church in Wilburn. Regardless of the confusion that may exist, we are most certain school was held in all the places listed even if the dates are not correct or debatable.

I want to begin this part of the school history during the fall of 1930 while the new building was being constructed. There were 5 or 6 high school boys that worked about an hour after school just cleaning up and doing any odd jobs for the contractor whose name was Sevier from Conway. The school was closed for one or two months early that spring of 1931 for lack of funds. There were 8 students in the 12th grade that year. The students were Buck Johnson, Virgil Abram, Elvis Spears, and Troy Barnett, Vernonia Stecker, Zora Butler, Essie Bostater, a girl from Clay or somewhere South East of Pangburn. She boarded with us for a short time and then moved in with Eva Cunningham, one of the teachers. They did not graduate. They did issue some sort of script, stating their records.

The law those days stated the loan had to be paid first. If there was money left sufficient enough to have school, then they had school. The county superintendent, then W. L. Deal, received the money from the state department. He and the school board then budgeted the money.

I must tell this story that happened most likely in 1933. They shut the school down in January, because there was not any money left after payment on the building loan. The building cost was $12,000. Some said it would never be paid. My sister Letta was teaching. She asked the school board to allow her to teach a subscription term of 2 months. She was granted that request, $1.00 per month tuition per student. She agreed to take about anything in payment whether it would be corn, cottonseed, hay, canned or dried fruit etc. The climax of this part of the story was a man that had three children in that subscription school. A total of $6.00 was due from this man. After school was out a few weeks, he sent word that he would pay in corn that was corn in shuck. Seventy-four pounds was standard measure for a bushel of corn in shuck. My sister told me to harness the mules and go get the corn. This old fellow couldn't read or write. We went to his crib where he had a big oak splint basket. We called it a shuck basket. It weighed 6 pounds. He had a mark on that old pivoting cotton scale at the 80-pound mark. We filled that basket hanging on the scales. When the scales balanced after he hung on the pen, then we emptied the corn into our wagon. He told me he owed for 3 bushels and a peck. Corn was 50 cents a bushel. I was 12 or 13 years old, but my math education told me something was wrong there, but I never mentioned it. When we had emptied the 3 bushels he stated he had always heard 100 big ears of com was a bushel, and asked me how many for a peck. I said 25. He then instructed me to help him pick out 25 big ears. When I got home I unloaded com in our crib and went to the house. My sister asked me how much corn I got. I told her, and she didn't frown or say a word.

I think it is appropriate to continue telling some school stories while on the subject of school. We had a boy in my class who was a quiet boy, very likeable, but I classed him sort of dumb. He never made a grade above 'C' and not often a 'C'. The grade of 'D' and 'F' was more likely. He didn't seem to mind getting bad grades. One day the teacher assigned a lesson to us students to bring to class a poem or rhyme the next day. This boy got up and started reading his poem. "Of all the fowls that roam the air, I'd rather be an owl. I'd fly upon the schoolhouse and listen to teacher's growl." The students were shocked at this boy's talent. Even though about 75 years have passed I recall that day very clearly. I think possibly the same year, we were assigned to bring to class a riddle. The late Paul Hazelwood, my age was a very good buddy of mine. He died at age 27 after going into the service. This was his riddle. "Up she jumped, out she ran and down she squatted, and out it come."

The teacher raised her voice to him. "What do you mean Paul?"

He replied, "Why that was just a girl who jumped up and ran out, squatted down and milked a cow." The class howled with laughter.

REX HARRAL: BOARD MEMBER
OF WILBURN SCHOOL
(As told to the author)

Rex was a board member of Wilburn School in 1947. The late Harvey Hazelwood, 1911–1980 was Principal of school. Harvey asked Rex to go with him to interview his Uncle John Wilson who was born 1872 and died in 1949. The old man was living in the log house he was born in and lived in all his life, located first residence part of Wilburn Creek going north on Dry Mountain road from Wilburn Community. The old man was sharp in memory. He rattled off all the information without hesitation. Harvey did not take notes, nor did I. Harvey wrote up the first history of Wilburn School for the first school year book in 1948 issue. Harvey resigned soon after that interview to enter college to become a Methodist Minister. Sileas Brewer, a high school teacher accepted the job of Principal of that term.

When the book came out, I bought a copy for my daughter Joyce. Upon reading the history Harvey had written, I was very proud of Harvey for the effort he had given to get that first yearbook in print of Wilburn School. I often wondered how long it may have before anyone would have done so, and by then possibly several older people had passed on. Upon reading the history of school that Harvey had written my memory of that interview of Uncle John soon discovered several errors. I don't recall just when after the book was out, that Harvey was home on a visit. I went up and had a great visit. I want to state here before going on in any discussion of this school history Harvey Hazelwood and I were life long friends, and I have no desire to ridicule Harvey in any manner. During our visit, I mentioned some things in that history I didn't agree with. Harvey immediately agreed he had made some grave mistakes. He further stated he had a deadline to meet when he wrote the history. He had a lot of things on his mind like getting off to college and stating it was in print and would just have to be that way.

I had already contacted several of older residents about the history of school, and had found there surely were some grave mistakes in the history of school in that yearbook. The late W. F. Uncle Billy Wessel, born in 1865 in Indiana, came to Wilburn in 1876. He fully agreed the first school was held at the old Terry Springs in an old log house once occupied by slaves. He wasn't sure how many terms there. But not long. He further stated he had no knowledge that Wilburn School was ever held at Center Chapel.

I think here is the proper time to discuss about Center Chapel school, the story of that building burning. First off that building was a Missionary Baptist church building. Typical of those days it was also a Missionary Baptist Church building. It was also a schoolhouse. I cannot gather any information when that building was built, but it was standing when the late Ottie Payton who was born and raised at what is now Center Ridge Road was the residence of O. L. Payton. He told me he started to school at Center Chapel in 1904, and the old church building was there then. The late George Ramsey, born in 1883 was blamed but never proven that he was the one that burned the Center Chapel Church house. George was an alcoholic. The late Oscar Chandler, born in 1898 told me he came by there just a year or so before George died one night. George and the late Jack Bradley were at the church and drinking heavily and had a fire going in the stove. George raked the fire out of the stove. Oscar told him he would burn the house down. Oscar scooped up and swept up all the fire and put it back in the stove and left, thinking he had no more business there with those drunks. The building burned down that night. That was the only evidence that George burned that building.

Both Ottie Payton and Oscar Chandler had no knowledge that Wilburn ever had school in that building. I discussed this with the late Jim Shearer born in 1879 and raised in this area. He had no knowledge that Wilburn ever attended school at Center Chapel building.

Soon after the church burned, a school was erected about a ½ mile north of church site, and school was held each year thereafter until 1926 or 1927. When Center Chapel School consolidated with Wilburn, the building was torn down and built into the Wilburn School building making a three-room school at Wilburn.

I wouldn't be happy with myself if I didn't include some of the major happenings during the history of the Wilburn community. I mentioned before that before a Wilburn Post Office was started, the community was called "Old Corinth."

In 1903 the late James (Uncle Jim) Baker was a prosperous merchant and community leader. He had a general merchandise store just west of the present day General Baptist Church. He gave the land for the church. Uncle Jim had applied for a post office. When he received an answer from his request, there were several people in the store as he opened up that letter. Someone asked him what he was going to call the post office. Someone suggested he call it 'Wilburn' after the nearby Wilburn Creek. He hesitated a moment, and then said, "Yes it will be Wilburn." My Uncle Alton 'Peg Leg' Johnson told me he was there at the very time Uncle Jim named the Wilburn Post office in 1903.

Uncle Jim lost his business from poor creditors. I knew Uncle Jim after he moved to Cooter Neck community. He was farming rented ground, and he still had a great reputation among his neighbors. I think his wife died in 1930. He gave up farming in 1931. He had failing eyesight for several years. He went to live with his son, Ray. He was totally blind at his death in 1933. Uncle Jim Shearer further stated according to his knowledge that they left the Terry Spring site and went to Old Liberty Church and was having school there as late as 1890.

The late Alton (Peg Lee) Johnson (1890–1968) went to school at Liberty in 1888. He didn't know when the church was built, but stated it burned in 1890 or so. He further stated he thought the Wilburn School was built north of Wilburn in 1890 or 1891, but wasn't quite sure. Most agreed they only had school in Dr. Tucker's building, no more than possibly the finished term after building burned and one year afterward, definitely not 9 years in the Tucker building.

The late Ottie Payton told me the old slave building was still standing in 1904 when he started to school at Center Chapel, but was falling down. He also stated the chimney was made of rock that was up so high and mud and small poles made up the final height, which was typical in those days.

I have done considerable research and dug deep into my memory, and I firmly believe what I have written is the very best and true history of Wilburn School and community. Harvey's wife Merle was high school English teacher and was respected and loved by students. Harvey had poor English in speech. I will always firmly believe that Harvey dictated the history to Merle and she wrote the history leaving more chance to error in the history of Wilburn School.

As I come to the end of my story of Wilburn, Arkansas, I am the oldest native of this community, having spent all but five of my 87 birthdays right here in Wilburn. I have researched to the very best of ability and am thankful for such a wonderful memory of my early life and my school days. It has enabled me to record this bit of history of Wilburn, Arkansas and its wonderful people that has been my privilege to have as great friends and neighbors.

Ever since I read the history of Wilburn School in the 1948 school annual, I have wanted to tell my side of it. When I had the opportunity to do so for this book, I was more than pleased.

This picture of Wilburn General Baptist Church was taken in 1950. A great effort has been made to identify the people in the picture. Those who have been identified are: Rex Harral, Gearldene Shearer, Bill Smith, Noel Staggs, Larry Southerland, Mack Shearer, Danny Shearer, Virginia Southerland, Bonnie Foust, Neva Ann Adams, Avene Gauvey, Patsy Stone, Mary Ann Varnum, Johnnie Lee Chandler, Lorene Holiman, Barbara Allen, Clotine Lafferty, Ella Smith, Gloria Ann Lafferty, Sharon Stone, Iris Taylor, Dorothy Smith, Betty Hazelwood, Marie Cockrum, Rosella Decker, Joyce Harrel, Georgia Fay Shearer, Rose Smith, Reginia Payton, Unfanell Holiman, Patsy Holiman, Dough Shearer, Gary Taylor, Butch Cockrum, Harrel Southerland, Aubrey Southerland, Paulette Southerland, Geneva Shearer, Joyce Southerland, Bill Foust, Curt Johnson, Alfred Foust, Alton Davis, Orwin Southerland, Gleman Nell Hayes, J.W. Foust, Ethel Foust, Darrel Southerland, Fern Holiman, Nicky Payton, John Dove, Jack Taylor, Leveta Cockrum, Juanita Cockrum, Elena Cockrum, Pansy Stonewalter, Goldie Ramsey, Beatrice Cockrum, James Cockrum, Mrs. Ledbetter, Birdie Stone, Joy Etta Cockrum, Eunice Shearer, Ruth Southerland, John D. Stone, Albert Hazelwood, Merle Adams, Paralee Smith, Cordia Allen, Bertha Taylor, Mona Ramsey, Alice Staggs, Mable Johnson, Mary Bell Southerland, Ima Jean Shearer, Velma Davis, Zora Shearer, Claudia Smith, Helen Payton, Cora McLester, Creasy Southerland, Dathel Shearer, Amy Butler, Jewell Harral, Dickie Harral, Vivian Holiman, Veda Foust, Winifred Southerland, Voyd Southerland, Molly Allen, Ezza Butler, Poter Butler, Jack Chandler, Faber Shearer, Elsie Adams, Nita Jo Adams, Estelle Shearer, Connie Floyd, Monroe Taylor, Alma Shearer, Amelia Southerland, Juanita Southerland, Edath Foust, Awin Hazelwood, Norma Lee Shearer, Osco Staggs, George Adams, Verlon Stone, Clinton Southerland, Loyd Stone, Loy Foust, Telford Allen, Sam Southerland, Wayne Foust, Lonnie Stone, Harrison Davis, Max Shearer, D.L. Southerland, Oather Payton, Willie Gage, Arvel Smith and Luther Floyd.

CASKET MAKING FOR THE DECEASED
(As told to the Author)

In the early days of the Wilburn community, burial caskets were hand-made. My maternal grandmother who was born in 1860 and died in 1942 told me some of the earliest burials in Magness Cemetery were buried in winding sheets and the deceased were wrapped in a sheet and buried. The late Rev. Uncle Will Foust was the casket maker of this community as far back as there is information. Most caskets were made of rough virgin yellow pine and hand planed and lined with whatever cloth was available. Uncle Will didn't have a shop. In case of rain he moved into his barn. Many neighbors volunteered to help. He often made the caskets and preached the funeral. During the WWI flu epidemic he made 12 caskets and preached 17 funerals. I can't recall who made the other caskets. This all happened in about 30 days. My mother lost 2 brothers, a sister-in-law and 2 small nephews, all in just 8 days.

The late Wyatt Roberson moved to this community in 1926 from Tyler. He was a journeyman carpenter, and set up shop in an old store building. He made most of the caskets. I helped him make several caskets myself. The last one was for Aunt Mary Butler. Wyatt was a Methodist minister. He too made many caskets and then preached the funerals, and seldom was paid. Someone that had the lumber stored in their barns that he had sawed for caskets many years earlier donated the lumber for those caskets. Neighbors dug graves by hand. I was helping someone find a grave in Center Chapel Cemetery once and somehow digging graves by hand came up. I got to looking and counted 27 graves in that cemetery I had helped dig. I can't recall just when digging graves by hand ended, but must have been in neighborhood of 1985 to 1990, and as might be expected some few kept digging by hand for several years after power digging started. It was common in those days of digging graves by hand that some women in the community would cook dinner for the grave diggers. Somehow the word would spread to the diggers to come to that woman's home for dinner. The scripture, "love thy neighbor as thy self" was well-honored in times of death. Food was brought to the family of the deceased in abundance. In those early days, there was a 'wake' set with deceased. No corpse was left alone the night after death. That wake was by members of the community, and just randomly selected and/or agreed among neighbors. Since there was no embalming of the deceased, burial had to be as soon as possible. In some cases in hot weather and certain causes of death, if the deceased died early in the day, every effort was made to have the funeral that afternoon.

Common bedding material was a straw tic, and material known as bed ticking was bought by yard enough to form a tick the size of the bed and filled with straw, but cornshucks was considered the best and had a much longer life than any straw but much more noisy. I recall several people marrying in the Depression who did not have money to purchase a mattress. They made a straw mattress to set up housekeeping. Pillows were always filled with feathers; most usually of duck or goose feathers yet chicken feathers were also used. I often heard about a 'crown' which was found in pillows of the deceased because the feathers were woven together to form a ball in the pillow. The story goes if the deceased was going to heaven that crown denoted the spirit of the deceased and told the resurrection of the deceased. Several years after my mother's death (I was nine at the time) that crown was found in my mother's pillow. I never did ask my sister that raised me and two sisters if this was true, something I regret now.

THE FIRST COTTON GIN
IN WILBURN

The first and only cotton gin in Wilburn arrived in 1896. It was hauled from Judsonia by wagon, the nearest railhead at that time. The power unit was steam powered. The boiler was dismantled and made up of units that was classed a one team wagon load. The largest part of the boiler was classed a 4 mule load. This cotton gin was set up a couple hundred yards north of the present Wilburn Fire Station. This caused quite a stir and people from the community were astounded at this happening.

Rex's maternal great grandfather Robert Fulton Johnson was born in 1834 and passed away in 1911. He had a blacksmith shop just across the street from the present day Wilburn post office. This old man was a master blacksmith and for those days a master of several trades that was typical of what blacksmiths did of that day. Upon unloading one of the gin stands they broke a heavy cast iron leg and brought it to "old Bob" as he was affectionately known and asked if he could make such a thing. He replied quickly, "No."

Then they asked, "Can you weld it?"

He looked at the thing several minutes and stated he might. They told him they needed it today. He replied it would take until tomorrow. The late Tom Batson told me this story. He said he was so curious to see how old Bob could do such a job that he hung around to watch. I am fully aware a lot of readers will have little knowledge of this part of the story. Welders will most likely understand.

Old Bob started making threaded rods to hold the pieces together while he heated this break in his forge that was heated with local made charcoal. He then sent someone down to Uncle Jim Baker's store, then located just west of the present day General Baptist Church. The person was instructed to get 2 lamp burners that was solid brass, that held the wick and globe that screwed into the top of those old kerosene lamps, the best source of illumination for that day. Old Bob cut those lamp burners into small pieces with his tin snips, and applied common Twenty-Mule Team Borax to the broken pieces, adding the small pieces of brass cut from those lamp burners, then bolted the pieces together with the threaded rods. It took 2 men to lift that heavy cast iron leg into the fire of his bellows powered forge. He then added about a bushel of charcoal and began slowly pumping the bellows, watching carefully how the heat was being distributed. After several minutes he had the whole thing red hot and he saw that brass now melted and running out of the joints. He well knew he had fused that large old piece of cast iron back together. He moved some of the charcoal back to reduce the heat gradually and let the cast-iron cool slowly. That was the first brazing job done in Wilburn, Arkansas.

Rex was Old Bob's great grandson, and later became the local blacksmith in the Wilburn Community.

One time Rex performed a brazing job just for novelty of it. He had a modern gas powered welding equipment, and just brazed some pieces of cast-iron. Those pieces burned in his shop in 1981. Brass melted and ran out destroying the subject. The gin was later moved to a location just across the street from Swint Tire Shop today. Typical of those days when a steam powered unit like that, if a gin was part of the business, a sawmill was also the main part, because the gin was only used during cotton harvest in the fall for about 3 months. A lot of set-ups in those days also had a gristmill that ground corn and wheat most likely on Saturdays only. I mentioned earlier about having a gristmill in our community. You simply had to live in a community with a gristmill to fully understand just how important the mill was, and how that mill linked neighbors. It soon became a socializing place in the community. There you learned about anyone that was sick or had serious problems. Some even swapped pocketknives, a deal that some thought was a purposeful trade.

Free range was all over these hills until after WWII. There were some ill feelings among some. A breech cow would ride fences and counties and get into the neighbor's fields. Some were nice and friendly and would work out problems. Seeing a cow with a steel yoke or forked tree branch around her neck told the story of her breaching. One man had a young team of mules that kept getting into a neighbor's cornfield. The neighbor finally got a full load of that foolishness. He loaded his shotgun and shot the mules up and had to pay a big fine.

Often a blacksmith's shop was part of the operation, making the operation a community hub. This gin went out of business in 1923 to 1924. I can only remember being their once with my dad. My dad bought a section of the building, tore it down and made a second corn crib. The sawmill only operated another year or so and quit. The late Uncle Will Staggs bought the gristmill and kept it in operation until 1937. He also had a shingle mill there until he sold the gristmill. That shingle mill would surely be a rare business today. This mill was a huge knife that went up and down by horsepower. The pine blocks preferably of virgin yellow pine was split into quarter blocks or so and boiled for an hour or so to soften them. They were then brought up by the knife (descendants of Uncle Bill was that old knife), a merry go round would be a good description of the mule powered source that brought that knife down that sliced off a shingle. A spring pole brought the knife back up, truly a pioneer operation. The late Ralph Johnson, a grandson of old Bob told me he remembered being at first sight of the gin. He said they had a steer that went round and round to press the cotton into bales. When they moved the gin they installed a more modem press that was powered by the steam engine.

I want to add more information to this cotton gin and sawmill story. They had a dug well for water source, as that steam boiler required a lot of water. One fall was dry and the well wouldn't furnish enough water. The late Bert Chandler, had a small pair of mules, he took contract to haul water from Wilburn creek just under the hill where Dry Mountain road crossed Wilburn creek. He made up a box of rough pine lumber, caulked the cracks and let water swell the lumber trying to make a water proof box to haul water. He never did get it to be really watertight. He really got himself a full time job. He drove the wagon out into the creek, used a bucket to dip the water. I don't know how many gallons that tank would hold, but using judgement, and the steepness of that hill the size of his mules tells me that most likely not much more than 100 gallons was a load. He pulled a plug when he got the wagon back up to the well, and soon was unloaded and back after another. He worked for days because there was no operating to keep them in water.

THE JERSEY COW

Only those that went through the great Depression of the 30's can truly evaluate the value of the jersey cow in all the family diet. At that time most of Arkansas was free range, meaning all livestock was running outside year around. The woods were burned off most every year and grass grew out in the woods. These abandoned fields were grazed to the ground. Cowbells were common appliances on at least one cow in each herd, so that each family could listen at home and tell where their cows were. If the cows didn't come home on their own, some family member had to go drive them home for milking. Most every family had more than one cow to milk. Families with large numbers often had five or 6 milk cows. This may be confusing to my readers of this day, thinking of the high production of today's dairy cows. The truth of the matter is that some of those cows never gave more than 2 gallons of milk daily. That milk had to be divided with her calf which nursed until it was several months old. Next was the fact no one fed that cow but little, especially in the summer months. Let me tell you about the common method of feeding a cow in the summer time. A cow would be fed one small ear of corn called a "nubbin" with shuck on, or maybe not anything. That cow just stood out in that open lot. First the calf nursed, and then was milked. The calf was separated for the night. After the cow was milked in the morning she was turned out on the free range again. Now if you are fully grasping my story, it may be a little easier to understand why that cow didn't produce any more milk then stated, but this was very common throughout the Ozarks of Arkansas. I can still see those poor old cows grazing now on that dried up grass so short I wondered how they got a bite. Their hollow guts told the whole story, and milking time confirmed the story.

There were other breeds of milk cows such as some called "milk Durham" which I think was probably milking short horn, and of course the cross breed bulls roamed the free range and cows just came in heat and most often the bull followed her home that night. The owners knew she was bred for another calf and dried her up in proper time for the next calving time. That meant that little effort was made toward improving the production of milk cows. Occasionally some one bought a young bull of better breeding, and all made some effort to get their cows bred to that bull. Yet a common expression was "a bull to bring milk" the next time.

Now to the cooks that are my readers: "Can you imagine feeding your family without one drop of milk in your kitchen? Have you ever tried making biscuits with water and baking powder? What did that cake look like without milk? Now I ask you, "Honestly and seriously dig deep into your imagination and truly try to think what it would be like to cook without milk. I can assure you there were some mothers that had that very task of feeding their families without milk or butter. I recall eating biscuits made without milk and I'm referring to biscuits made from plain flour. She added baking powder. Those old gals brushed up on their cooking skills and made biscuits that were acceptable anywhere. But try to bake cornbread from home ground meal without milk. I never knew of any cook that became famous for cornbread made without milk. It was more like going camping today comparing those cooks today. There was no refrigeration, dry beans, fat back salt meat, or potatoes.

I recall one family who had two milk cows that were accidentally poisoned. That was during the depths of the Depression, with simply no money to buy a cow, and the bank had loaned all that man could possibly repay at harvest time. Again I ask you, dig deep into your imagination to feel what it was like living in those days. A common utensil for milking was the 8-pound lard pail so common in every home. I still have a mental picture of one family of about 6 children, every kid old enough to milk headed toward the milking lot with each carrying an eight pound bucket, and after milking that bucket was only about half fall. I can't imagine today trying to care for that milk without refrigeration. Those with dug wells often hung that milk down in that well to keep it cool, some had holes dug on north side of the building called a milk well that provided some refrigeration, yes some were energetic and full of energy. Perhaps a way to describe that generation, "a breed of their own who made do with meager things, but a brain with common sense."

It would be a great treat today to sit down to a breakfast table of those old cooks with their homemade biscuits, a big bowl of home churned butter, home made wild muscadine jelly, sorghum molasses, and homecured ham. Well that's enough to make your mouth water isn't it? Many lived like that, but those without that family milk cow, again use all your imagination, and you will still be short of the real thing trying to survive without milk and butter. The family that lost all their cows by poisoning had a girl my age. She is still living. Recently we were talking and she said, "I can't tell you how hungry we got. It was during crop time and yet we were hungry for better food. It's hard to describe how great it was when a sympathetic neighbor loaned us a cow to milk. We had milk and butter again on our table, even though we seldom had milk to drink it was great to cook with."

In winter months feeding the cows wasn't much different than summer months, only more feed. For those that grew cotton most often fed the cottonseed. About 1500 pounds of seed cotton (picked out of the field) was called a bale. When ginned the lint cotton bale was about 500 pounds, leaving about 1000 pounds of cotton seed which was high in protein and fat which could be sold at the gin but most kept the seed for planting next spring and cow feed during the winter. Some added a nubbin or two to the cottonseed. Most people were very particular about feeding their mules and horses for the team was the very bottom of their transportation and other power needs. A well fed team and poor milk cows was a common sight during the Depression in the Ozarks. Today I often go to the local school and churn butter by shaking the cream in a gallon jar. I don't think the kids (elementary) ever manage to understand why the milk (cream) can be liquid, and after a few minutes of shaking becomes a solid butter on a cracker. This is something they never get at home.

Today I sometimes have fresh milk for sale, illegal to sell, but some feel they get a product that is healthy and some tell me that they won't drink store bought pasteurized milk. It just lacks the flavor they get from raw milk, but enjoy the fresh unpasterized milk.

THE OLD LOG HOUSE WILSON HOME HAD MANY MEMORIES

The late James H. Wilson started this log house in 1862. He got the logs erected and ready for the roof, but joined the Confederate Army before it was finished. Upon returning from the Civil War, he finished building the house and married his girlfriend, Julia. They had four children, John in 1872, Aggie in 1874, Edna in 1877 and Willie in 1879. Vandals burned their log house around 1982. John lived his entire life there. He only spent one night away from home. He caught the M&NA train at Pangburn, rode to Helena, spent the night and caught the same train home the next day.

Their sons John and Willie never married. They both became widely renowned blacksmiths. They did work oddities in the simple log building that was unheard for blacksmiths. They both had a particular liking to making guns. The early guns often had lever type main springs and those springs did break. The father John would often take an old worn out file and forge a new spring for a gun. John was a fiddler and made his own fiddle and once he decided he didn't like the tone of his fiddle, so he just made another one and gave the old one to a good friend. Both sons made many gunstocks out of walnut. They cut the tree, split and dried the timber in their small shop. Some of that stock was thirty years old, and a lot of dry walnut was in the attic when both died, just a few months apart. Both liked corn squeezings they made themselves, but neither became alcoholics. No one was able to buy any of their fire water, but if you were good friends you were welcome to a big swig. If John got a little too much of the squeezings he became very unruly and would get out his knife if someone tried to quiet him. Willie would scold him and tell him to settle down and he would be quiet.

THE SWINGING BRIDGE AND MOONSHINING

The Author's Notes: This book would not be complete if the author did not have the permission to include three of Rex's most noteworthy and published stories.

The late John and Willie Wilson brothers had built a swinging footbridge across Wilburn Creek at the present site of today's concrete two-lane traffic bridge. They used a big steel cable anchored to a large tree on each side, which was several feet above normal flow of the creek. We teenage boys loved to go swimming in that baptizing hole. During high waters after a rain, we often jumped off that bridge into those raging waters and swam down to stiller waters and swam out and repeated our fun. The old bridge held up for a long time.

As stated earlier, the General Baptist Church was originally a 2-story building and a lodge hall located in the upper story. The entrance to the lodge hall was a stairway from outside. The late J. W. (Uncle Will) Foust was pastor for many years. Moonshiners became strong for a few years. One night Uncle Will was preaching during a revival.

Some of the most mischievous boys went upstairs and poured some of their "corn Squeezings" down through the cracks in the floor that landed on the old preacher. He just moved over and said, "Boys will be boys." Then he went back to his preaching.

I haven't been able to determine what year the telephone came to Wilburn. Of course it was a party line, and in some cases almost a nuisance as each patron was at a certain day of the month to check the line and see that the line was working. As might be expected that didn't work out very well as the line was often nailed to trees, and many times during a rain the wet limbs of the trees dropped down on the line and shorted it out. Many other things kept the line out of order. Also the party line meant several people were on that same line. Each person had a certain ring and that ring went into all phones on that line.

Everyone soon learned other family's rings, and lots of eavesdropping went on and that soon caused friction among neighbors. I was only four or five years old when they took out the old party line, but one incident still lingers in my mind just like it was yesterday. My mother was talking to a neighbor lady, when the lady said, "Oh! I must hang up. Can't you smell my green beans scorching?" My mother often told that story. I'm sure that was her favorite story.

Oscar Chandler owned the first car in Wilburn. I was told it was a 1920 Dodge touring car. I have only faint memories of that car. The late Ellis Ramsey bought the Farmers Mercantile Store when Mack Butler sold out and moved to Pangburn. Soon after Ellis took over he bought a model T Ford one ton. This rig had no top, but was a heyday over hauling freight from Heber Springs over a wagon and team. I recall hearing his oldest son telling someone he made two trips to Heber, about 10 miles in one day and hauled as much or more than any wagon and team could haul. That was progress back in those days.

Moon shining became quiet an enterprise in this community. I recall hearing my Uncle Peg Leg Johnson telling how he stood on Main Street in Wilburn as he called it and could see the smoke of six liquor stills north of Wilburn. After prohibition days, some were determined to keep on making it as there was a good demand for the "squeezings."

Naturally the Fed agents soon made a visit to the community. A couple was arrested and ended in the penitentiary. One was released and in those days the gates were open and the man was on his own to get home. I heard this story when I was just a just a kid, and thought it was a hoax. Later in life 1 learned it was true. It was getting dark when this man reached home. I suppose he had in his mind to test his wife's character. In those days everyone hollered at the gate, "Hello!" He changed his voice a bit and his wife, Laury, came to the door. It was too dark for her to recognize him and he asked to stay the night. She replied, "No, just me and the children are here." He opened the gate and started toward the house and said, "1 must have a place to sleep." She reached behind the door and came out with a double-barreled shotgun. He immediately replied, "Laury, Laury, this is Ed."

There is a whole book of the stories about moonshining. Sometime in the 30's a couple of single boys were making illegal spirits and were worried about hauling it around in their model T Ford. They decided to let air out of their spare tire and put some pint bottles in the tire and install the flat tube and then air up the tire, having the bottles hidden inside their spare tire. It worked until they had a flat on one tire. They were on a busy road and several friends stopped to help. When they got the flat off, the friends wanted to know why they didn't install the spare and get going. One finally got the smarts and said he didn't think the spare was durable.

*Definition: Moonshining: Pertaining to whiskey unlawfully made or smuggled.

FISH GIGGING

I find it very difficult to recall just how primitive we lived in my childhood days, just how hard we had to work, and how we learned to do without. We simply made do, or did without. Our food simply came from what we made and grew at home, again we made do or did without. Yet in my time we had much more than my parents. We had the old pressure cooker that enabled us to can any kind of meat and many more vegetables that made our diet much more balanced than my forefathers had.

I wonder if I can give my readers a real mental picture of what life was like in those pioneer days before our present means of growing and preserving our foods. When there was only salt to preserve meats, then that meant you ate the fresh slaughtered meat, before it spoiled, or in the event of winter weather, it was salted and sometimes smoked so that it would keep for months. Beans and peas were left on the vine until they dried, and were picked by hand, and often shelled by hand and sometimes picked and left in burlap sacks lying out in the sun till they were really dry. Then perhaps the younger kids got to exercise by jumping and tramping on those sacks until the shells were crushed, then the beans or peas were winnowed to separate the hulls, then stored. Of course green beans were sometimes strung on strings to dry and com was cut off the cob and dried. Yet, I doubt my readers can truly realize just how much time it took to preserve foods in those days. If you hear some older person state, "we toiled from sun to sun," you just have to think what it was like.

In those truly pioneer days, people more or less lived off the land. I mean when spring came, there was wild greens, dandelions, poke, lambs quarter etc., that was picked and consumed. This was a real treat from dry beans and salt pork. Of course there was lots of meat in the woods on hoof such as deer, squirrel, turkey, rabbits etc. I almost gag when I think about the possums I have ate in my time, but it took time to harvest those wild meats.

All the streams in Cleburne were filled with all kinds of fish. Not only was fish a part of their diet, everyone liked fish. Anyway from using a pole and hook to capture fish to hogging, which was mostly done after the small streams were about dried up, then wading and feeling under rocks and logs and catching fish by hand. I never got hooked on that kind of fishing. I was too afraid of catching a snake, and some did get bit too.

My favorite way of fishing was gigging fish. We waited until the creeks or the river was low, and of course, the water was warm and we could wade when necessary. Every local blacksmith could make a gig. Some were more gifted than others in making gigs. One local blacksmith had the title of making the best gig. He often made his gigs from old car springs, even an old horse shoeing rasp was a choice piece of scrap metal to make a gig. It took about a half day's work to make a good gig. Some forged the handle socket right on the gig, which made a choice gig and perhaps the strongest way. Others made the gig with a tine and used the ferrule from an old hoe handle to cap the gig handle.

The handle was usually made from a piece of straight grained pine board ripped to about one inch square and then rounded with a draw knife and scraped by hand with a pocket knife. Most tied a strong string to the gig itself and then wrapped the string around the handle which was about eight foot long with a small hole in the top of the handle. The string was run through that hole, in the event he wanted to throw the gig at a fish, he still had a hold on the gig and could retrieve his gig and hopefully a fish too.

However, most fish were gigged with the handle in the operator's hand, and held to the bottom while the fish weakened or died.

Gigging was done at night. For a light, we made a wire basket from old hay wire and sometimes combining a piece of hog wire, interlaced with hay wire. The last basket I made for a gigging light, I used the rod from the rim of an old set of bed springs. This rod was about a quarter of an inch in diameter. I salvaged this rod, cut off about four feet, made a ring and forge welding the ends together making the ring about sixteen inches in diameter.

Then the art of weaving of wire to make a basket about eighteen to twenty inches in depth. I used a piece of old wagon tire to make a stand that was bolted to the front end of the boat about four feet high, and leaning out from the boat about a couple of feet. Now I've got your attention, "what was this basket for?" For a light we used 'fatty' pine, or rich pine.

We often took the old cross cut saw, got down on our knees and cut off those old pine stumps that were full of pitch and would bum like they were soaked in kerosene or other fuels. We split those pieces down about two inches in diameter.

We almost had a boatload when we got the front end loaded with that fatty pine. I hope my readers can feel the pain of those old aching arms and backs as we cut these old stumps and split them up to our needs. When we got the boat in the water, we started a fire with that fatty pine and kept about three of four pieces burning in that basket at all times. This made an ideal light. It was a yellow light that didn't make a glare or glint to the water like a bright light would do. Of course, there was that fog of black smoke coming off that burning fatty pine. We sometimes looked like a coal miner when we finished our nights gigging.

FROG GIGGNG IS A NIGHT AFFAIR

Rex got more comments and phone calls than he ever received on this story when it was published in 'The Sun Times.

Frog gigging is done with a boat and at night. However, frogs can be found along any body of water be it a pond, creek or whatever: We look for that white belly shining as it sits on the bank or a log, or a stump. Any kind of light is sufficient as long as the light is bright enough to shine the banks and show that white frog belly.

Last summer, one evening just about sundown, I was settled down to read the daily paper when two teenage boys drove up in a pickup with a boat in the back. They approached me with a question. "Aren't you an old pro at gigging frogs?"

I replied, "I don't know as I'm an old pro, but have gigged a lot of frogs in my time."

"Well then, come with us and show us how," they said.

The first thing I asked was, "how late you staying out?"

"We will come home anything you say," they said.

"Well, I will go with you then," I replied.

When I got in the cab with those boys, I soon discovered they had been partaking of "corn juice", or "corn squeezings." When we unloaded the boat at the creek, that bottle of corn juice showed up. I told the boys that corn juice just had to lie in the boat if I was going. They agreed. I paddled the boat and we started down the creek, picking up a couple of nice frogs as we went. All was going well, the boys were a little excited, especially with that corn juice being a helper.

We came to a large old stump sitting in the edge of the water. I told the boys we could surely expect a frog around that old stump. I eased the boat up to the stump, and started easing around when one boy said, "I don't see any frogs but there is a large moccasin laying over there."

I said, "Gig him!"

He replied, "No, I'm not going to catch him." I yelled at him to gig that snake and keep his hands to himself. He replied, "No, he ain't going to bite no one, he has a frog in his mouth."

I then realized he had more of that corn juice than I thought.

Just then he grabbed that old snake around the neck, and that snake wrapped around his arm squirming, and me yelling, "turn that thing loose!" After about a minute, which seemed like ten, that old snake let go of that frog. Now the snake had his mouth wide open, that old cottonmouth shinning like the moon.

I'm still yelling for him to turn that thing loose. About then, one of the others said, "Hey! He wants some of that corn juice." He reached down and got that bottle and poured a shot of that juice down that gaping mouth before dropping the snake into the water. I was disgusted but at least he didn't have that snake in his hands anymore. I was relieved of that worry and I was telling them in no uncertain means, there would be no more snake capturing tonight. I was paddling along again when I heard a little noise behind me. I looked around and behold, there was that old moccasin with a frog that he had caught in his mouth and wanting to trade that frog for more corn juice!

THE LAND OF CALIFORNIA MOUNTAIN

California Mountain is one of the best-kept secrets in Northern Arkansas. The Mountain shelters the communities of Prim, Woodrow, Everett, Sunny Slope, Poff Mountain, and Brewer. These communities have not lost their identity as the vastness of the growing cities, which are surrounding it. The little group that settled in this small community were the ones who made the place the individual and significant place that it is. It was and still is a closely knitted religious community, and their lives revolve around the one school, churches and the historical gem, the Everett Cemetery behind the little historical wooden schoolhouse. Most of the people who live here are kin to one another.

Some of the original inhabitants of Prim are, the Knapps, the Carltons, Everetts Hipps, and the Stubbs are buried in the historical Everett cemetery. Some family names in the area are the Aldridges, Brewers, Gates, Cox, Carrolton, Davis, Everett, Finch, Hall, Hazlewood, Hunt, Prim, Pettit, Poff, Six, Smart, Stevens, Smith, Vanada, Verser and Whitaker.

California Mountain is a meandering country farming village, which has kept its old-timey ways staying within its own land and people. Truly this little village has a special enchantment of its own.

THE PROFILE
OF BESS KNAPP

Bess Knapp and her husband WC are long time residents of the Prim area of Cleburne County, Arkansas. They are known throughout California Mountain that their lives are embodied by the principles of God's Word. They belong to the Prim Full Gospel Holiness Church. In the eyes of their children and friends they are known as a devoted husband, wife, and mother and father. They have 4 children and several grandchildren. Bess and WC have been instrumental in donating the land for the church and school working behind

the scenes in Prim. WC owns the Knapp Hardware store in Prim. Bess is a renowned historian and is called upon many times for history on the area of California Mountain. Bess finds the history of California Mountain fascinating and has documented much of what she has learned through the years. She has recorded much of the history of Prim, Brewer, Sunny Slope and Everett, The Ridge and all apart of California Mountain. She has a praiseworthy collection of the history of Northern Arkansas in her home office. Bess is known as a published author and historian. One of her books is called 'Stories, People, and Cemeteries of the Communities of Brewer, Prim, Woodrow, Everett Ridge, and Sunny Slope. She and her daughter, Jane who is a Spanish teacher at Heber Springs High School, are writing a book on the history of California Mountain. They want to make sure the history does not get lost and will be passed on to future generations. As a long time member, Bess assists the Historical Society from time to time in helping people from all over the nation—who in some way are connected to the milk and honey land of California Mountain.

Bess never knows who will be knocking at her door to get information, which this well brought up lady gives ungrudgingly. She has given speeches to The Historical Society and various clubs. This lady has contributed so much to Arkansas, making sure that future generations will never forget the exciting saga and mysteries of California Mountain, which includes the mysterious round boulders, the 'Yellow Bluffs' and buried treasurers, etc. She knows pretty much everyone in 'California Mountain' because of her four decades as postmaster at Prim. Some people refer to her as 'the matriarch of 'California Mountain'.

Bess Knapp was born April 2, 1927 at Woodrow, Arkansas to Fate and Lillie (Hipp) Stevens. She was the fifth sibling in a line of eight. She had two brothers, Warren and Johnny and 5 sisters. Hazel, Ruby, Mildred, Freda, and Shelby Jean whom at this time (2007) are all still living. Bess graduated from a 2-room grade school called Woodrow School. When it was time for her to go to high school, there weren't any buses that ran from Woodrow to Heber Springs, so she boarded there during her time in Heber Springs High School. On Sundays, they attended church in the same building the children did their school lessons during the week. Back then they didn't have full-time preachers. When anyone came to hold revival or preach on Sunday their dad took them in a mule driven wagon.

Bess was a shy young beautiful dark haired girl who had an adventurous spirit. She loved God and enjoyed helping others, and she was always intensely interested in the history of her family and community. She and her sisters enjoyed singing together and sang at churches and other events. The highlight of their singing came when the historical Gem Theater in Heber Springs had them perform. In 1942 when WW II was on, Bess went to Eureka, Missouri near St. Louis to live with her sister Hazel and her husband, Howard Carlton. While there this soft-spoken young girl worked at a company that made 30 and 50 caliber shells. When her sister's husband was drafted into the Navy, Bess and her sister returned to Prim.

Later that year Bess with her sister Hazel and cousin Marguerite traveled to Seattle, Washington where Hazel's husband was stationed. The women were very excited as they boarded the Missouri and North Arkansas train at Edgemont and traveled to Joplin, Missouri where they exchanged trains and continued on to Seattle.

At the time the U. S. government's propaganda campaign was encouraging women to join the war effort. Widespread male enlistment left vacancies in essential industries such as airplane and munitions production and nearly 3 million women answered their country's call to serve in defense plants. At first there was lots of reluctance on the parts of managers, husbands, male workers, and many women against doing this work. But America was at war, and women were needed. While Howard served in the Navy, Bess and her sister worked at the Boeing Aircraft in Seattle building B-29 bombers. Bess' job at Boeing was riveting. At that time, the popular song Rosie the Riveter was written by Redd Evans and John Jacob and was one of the best-known patriotic songs to keep the morale up for everyone.

Bess worked at the Hager Hinge Company also. When the war was over, Bess didn't fall down to the prewar levels. She returned to Prim, Arkansas and married her childhood sweetheart WC Knapp. County

Judge, Elbert Smith who was from Prim united Bess and W.C. in marriage at Heber Springs.

In June of 1947, WC's father gave them a farm. It was located in Stone County on Hanover Road, about a ½ mile off Highway 263. WC worked in timber in the area, but also planted six acres of cotton on his land. However, the boll weevils got the best of the cotton crop, so in August of each year, they traveled to Indiana to pick tomatoes for two months and then returned to Prim.

In 1951 WC and Bess purchased the Prim General Store from Julian and Mildred Carlton, one of Bess's sisters. That same year Bess was commissioned as Postmaster. She got to know almost everyone on the Mountain during her four decades as postmaster at Prim. She filled that position at Prim for the next 40 years, retiring on August 31,1990. Her daughter Darlene is now the postmaster of the Prim Post Office.

In 1953 WC went to St. Louis, Missouri and worked at the Ford and Mercury plant while Bess stayed home to take care of her four children and run the store and post office. WC returned to Prim in 1955 to help operate the store and raise chickens. They gave the store to daughter Janie and her husband Douglas in 1963. Bess continued on as Postmaster and WC continue to raise chickens and other critters from time to time.

In 1979 WC and Bess purchased the building supply store in Prim from Odis Hipp. They renamed it Knapp Building Supply. It is still on the main street in Prim. Bess and WC had four children, Jane, Bill, Darlene and Bobby Neal who all live nearby. Her youngest son, Bob Knapp and his wife Kathy Jo own a Truss Company in Prim. Their oldest son, Bill Knapp and his wife Mary own a 3,000-acre ranch with 1,000 cattle and four chicken barns. Bess enjoys visiting with their children and attending church.

THE WINKLEY BRIDGE

✦

(Compliments of The Sun Times, written by Chastine Shumway)

A summary of the historical Cleburne County Swinging Bridge: The Winkley Bridge, known as the 'Old Swinging Bridge' was built in 1912, closed to vehicles in 1971 and made the National Register of Historic Places in May 1985. The pastoral bridge was dedicated to the Arkansas State Historical Society May of 1986 when it was placed on the National Register for Historic Places. The well known rustic brown colored suspension bridge was featured in national *Coca-Cola* television advertisements in 1987 and 1988 and written up in the *Southern Living magazine, U.S. news*

and World Report serving as the scene for a group portrait of the Arkansas Symphony Orchestra. It was special to people here in Cleburne County.

This bridge hung between towers on opposite banks of Little Red River and giant cables supported the structure. It is believed that the engineers who designed the bridge were the same ones who designed and built the Golden Gate Bridge in San Francisco, California in the 1930s. Construction was started on May 27, 1912 and the bridge was finished in November of the same year. It was 550 feet long and for more than two generations was the only convenient link between the eastern section of the county and Heber Springs. According to some Cleburne County residents, the bridge was condemned some time before 1930. In 1968 a delegation of Cleburne County citizens asked the Arkansas Highway Commission to replace Winkley Bridge and to designate it as a tourist attraction. The proposal was approved and the Arkansas Highway Department programmed the Winkley Bridge for replacement July 24, 1968. The bridge became a tourist attraction and stood as a symbol of the Little River's history in the development of Cleburne County.

Saturday, October 28, 1989: Many youths were attending an annual church fellowship meeting that started Thursday, October 26th and would last four days at the Prim Holiness Church in Prim. About 300 people came from other states and cities to attend this special meeting and were from Mississippi, Alabama, Oklahoma and Kentucky. A walk on the swinging bridge was a traditional outing for this church youth group, and they always looked forward to this eventful time with their friends. Gayla Carlton was the daughter of Vernon Carlton, pastor at that time of the church. She was 34 years of age and had agreed to watch over the group when they went to the Bridge. This would be the last time anyone would swing on the 'old swinging bridge'. The little Red River would be a watery grave for some of them. The Swinging Bridge was 50 to 60 feet above the Little Red River with scenic rock formations on each side. On this soon to be a tragic day, some 40 to 50 people were swinging on the bridge.

Jennifer Johnson, a witness who lived three miles east of the bridge said she was driving to her home about three miles from the bridge when she noticed it swinging wildly. She said she stopped and remarked to a friend that the bridge was swinging higher than she had ever seen it swing before. "We used to swing on the bridge ourselves when we were kids but we never swung it near as high as they were doing." she said. The bridge was swinging when its upstream side appeared to buckle. It turned upside down and tumbled into the Little Red River. People at each end of the bridge were running towards the edge in an attempt to get off the falling bridge. As the bridge fell, some of the people were just running in the air, and flung around like rag dolls. On this heartbreaking day it was a matter of seconds before everyone was in the water. As the bridge plunged into the water, screams of terror and prayers filled the air. The well-built bridge, which was constructed of wooden timbers, did not break apart when it fell into Little Red. Rescue workers had to cut the bridge apart in 10-foot sections to retrieve the bodies buried beneath it.

Pastor Zachary Generaux of the Prim Holiness church said they expect 100s of people from all over the southern states to visit this 52nd annual camp meeting. There will be several ministers teaching the 'Word' and there will be many testimonies from people. There will be some discussion about the happening of the swinging bridge and their loved ones. Some people will bring their musical instruments, and there will be lots of home-made food served. Some will make their annual journey to visit the site of the tragedy where a cement memorial marker, which was part of the bridge, has been placed.

Jason Carlton, a survivor who was and still is the local Greers Ferry barber, remembers this happening well because he was with the Prim church group on the bridge and was lucky to be a survivor. When the bridge cables snapped, it flipped over, throwing everyone into the water. One cable on the Wilburn side broke, and on the Heber Springs side, a cable on the opposite side broke, making the bridge twist instead of actually flipping. The bridge fell killing five and injuring many others. Jason said, "It landed on me."

Frank Valentine, a fireman, was one of the first to arrive on the scene after the collapse. He performed CPR on him, and Carlton is alive today because of his quick action. Jason said, "The good Lord let me come back. Others weren't as lucky."

Valentine said he and some other rescue workers used a jack to free a young girl and a man who were under the bridge. He then devoted his attention to Gaila Carlton, the minister's daughter who was trapped in the river but to no avail. Melvin Decker of Heber Springs, a Hopewell Volunteer Fire Dept member was among many others who helped people from the river also.

Jason said, "There were three young ladies, Gayla Carlton of Prim, Dana Waltman of Van Cleve, Mississippi, and Catrina Cotwell, of Stratford, Oklahoma, and two guys, Jason Williams of Muldrow, Oklahoma and David Shane Warren, of Mayfield, Kentucky killed." Carlton recalled one person who lost his sister. "He was standing there, telling people to help his sister. She was just a few feet away, but could not be helped."

Once people started looking, they found the two broken cables. There was no indication anything would have gone wrong. It has been surmised that the bridge had about 40 to 50 young people swinging on it. In the animation of the moment they did not realize what was happening as they swung the bridge higher and higher. The old bridge could not sustain it.

Deputy Andy White said the Rust Company, which was working on a highway bypass project nearby was instrumental in the rescue effort. The company brought several pieces of heavy road equipment and lights to the scene. The local restaurant furnished blankets and food.

Life goes on and the 52nd annual fellowship camp meeting will be held on the last full weekend in October at the Prim Holiness Church. Everyone is welcomed. In the foyer of this picturesque church nestled in the Ozark Mountains, is a glass case hanging with the pictures of the people who lost their lives that day. Sister Tina Williams, mother of Jason Williams, age 16, who lost his life, wrote a heart-felt poem, which hangs in the case. It is a memorial to that haunting day 'lest we forget'.

THE RENDEZVOUS
By Sister Tina Williams

About 3:30 in the afternoon,
A snow-white angel band, was dispatched
From the glory world, to earth, mortal's land
As our five children, on the bridge, unknowingly,
Soon to be gone. A heavenly host,
At God's command, swept down,
To take them home.
I can see them now, in glorious splendor,
Stretched flat in flight, they flew,
Did not come for all that day,
But as commanded, just a few,
And tho we weep and miss them sore,
At times it's hard to bear,
Blessed saints and many friends, have in
Our sorrow shared.
But grief and tears turn to joy, we
Realize, 'twas no mistake,
One moment our dear ones on the Swinging Bridge,
The next moment, inside heaven's gates.
They left this testimony that they pleased
The Lord. "What more could we ask?
And God in infinite wisdom, gave them rest
From earthly task,
"Don't worry for our sorrow, loved ones,
For we have received grace.
Just watch the entrance closely, children,
Because it won't be long,
In answer to your beckoning, we, too, are coming home.

And so Gaila, Jason, Katrina, Dana, and David,
Keep the gates swung wide,
For the rapture of the glorious reunion,
Waiting just inside."

The community not only lost a treasured landmark, but loved ones also who met their destiny with God at The Little Red.

CALIFORNIA MOUNTAIN BOY HERO IN WWII

Loyd and his girlfriend, Ernestine Carlton attended school together before he went into the service. When he came home they were married in 1946. They had three children, Beverly Pitts, Everly Kellar and Tim Stubbs. He, like many others, left as a green country boy to fight for his country and returned as one of the heroes in WWII from California Mountain. He passed away March 12, 2002.

In 1941 Loyd Stubbs fought in the 96th Combat Division, commonly referred to as the DeadEye Division which fought valiantly in the Philippines. The 96th Division fought Japan in the final stages of WWII and became a part of the liberation force. This Division included several men from the Woodrow area. It was only one of four Divisions to receive the Presidential Unit Citation. The 96th produced 5 Medal of Honor Winners, one of which was presented for an infantryman from Fayetteville, Arkansas. Loyd had been previously awarded the Combat Medal, Purple Heart and now the prestigious Bronze Star was added in August of 2005. LTC Gray said Loyd was also entitled to four other medals and ribbons that were not presented previously. These were The Asiatic Service Medal, the WWII Victory Medal, The Ruptured Duck Ribbon, and the Philippines Liberation Ribbon. These medals were forwarded to his wife Ernestine on Loyd's behalf. The Bronze Star is presented only to those infantrymen who served in the trenches and were the last ones to leave the scene of a battle. It is awarded to those who distinguished themselves in battle by a heroic or meritorious achievement.

THE BARE FACTS ABOUT
BLACK BEARS IN PRIM

✦

*(Compliments of The Sun Times, written by
Chastine Shumway)*

Arkansas was known as the Bear State in the 1800s because of the state's
black bear abundance. In fact, game of every description was abundant,
crystal-clear fish filled rivers, remote hills, and acres of timberland, which
was perfect habitat for these mammals to make their home in.

The Indians who lived here thought bears were healers and keepers of
spiritual well being. As the bears hibernated in the winter in trees, caves
and mountains the Indians hunted and harvested them. The bear and
other game was the red man's survival kit. Therefore all parts of the bear

was utilized. Meat and fat were a delicacy, the skins were used for clothing, and the claws and teeth were made into jewelry and medicinal remedies. Bearskins were traded to explorers and settlers.

By the late 1920s bears dwindled due to overhunting. Arkansas prohibited hunting in hopes of restoring the animal population.

In 1949, the Arkansas Game and Fish Commission made a decision to reestablish the species. More than 250 bears were brought in from Canada and Minnesota and were relocated in the Ozarks to help solve this problem.

Game and Fish ecologist Rick Eastridge of Conway was the guest speaker at a recent meeting of the Audubon Society's Fairfield Bay chapter. He said, "The program has become "one of the most successful large carnivore re-introductions in the United States."

"I've always been intrigued and curious about bears, even as a boy. I remember seeing a picture of my father hand-feeding a bear in the Great Smoky Mountains National Park. I always wondered how he could do that because I had the impression that they would attack a person." He continued saying, "Usually if they see you, they will lumber away. I had many misconceptions about bears and while in college, I took advantage of opportunities to learn about them. My studies eventually led me to a great career with Arkansas Game and Fish Commission."

He estimates the state's bear population at 3,500, including several in Cleburne County. There is considerable interest in the Cleburne County area as bear sightings have been reported recently in Drasco, Edgemont, Fairfield Bay, Prim, etc. At Prim, John and Joyce Carlton took pictures of a 300 pound bear robbing their bird feeder. In Drasco a bear was harvested recently by a man who was deer hunting.

"We don't attempt to estimate the bear population on a county level. We estimate the bear population on a regional level. We have approximately 2,000 or more bears in the Ozark mountain region now. Cleburne County definitely has a few bears but not a lot. Arkansas does not have the feared grizzly bears, only the black bears." He noted that the black bear could be cinnamon brown, with white markings too.

Only one bear was harvested in Cleburne County during the 2002 bear-hunting season, and two bears the year before. The top counties in terms of harvest were Pope (30 bears harvested), Desha (29 bears harvested) and Johnson (25 bears harvested). In 2001, 46 bears were killed in Newton County, 38 in Johnson, and 30 in Desha County. "So based on the bear harvest results, we must assume that Cleburne County does not have an over-abundant number of bears," said Eastridge.

Should residents be worried about them? "Bears have a very keen sense of smell. If they get the scent of a human, they usually avoid them. The most dangerous time to be near a bear is when she is with cubs. That's when the mother stands upright, because she knows her cubs are in danger, and she's ready to protect them," the biologist said.

"If a bear starts after you, don't run. Start flapping your arms and make a lot of racket. Above all don't play dead or try to outrun them. Bears can run 30 miles an hour, climb great heights, and swim well," he said.

Bears are carnivores and eat flesh of mammals, but their main diet is vegetation such as persimmons, acorns, hickory nuts, leaves and buds, and berries. "If you think you have a bear visiting your property, check trees for bear hair, as they use trees for back scratchers. Also check for footprints. A bear has 5 toes. Habituated bears are extremely dangerous, so don't encourage them with food," Eastridge instructed. "Their favorite dessert is honey. In fact the Indians called the bears, "sticky fingers." "If you have a hive or several hives it is wise to install an electric fence around them. This discourages the bears. In the long run an electric fence will save you time and money. "If you spot one, you can identify the female by the small Mickey Mouse ears and a sagging belly", he added.

Eastridge added that the only time the female and male bear tolerate each other is mating time, which is between May and August. "They hibernate in a den, which might be a cavity, cave, big tree, or mountain ledge, in June and July for about eight weeks. Black bears, unlike other species, get up and down and wander around during their part-time hibernation. The female bear has 2 to 5 cubs. This differs in all areas. When their cubs are born they grow very fast. The newly born cubs weigh around 8 ounces or less. They are born blind, toothless, and covered with fine hair. They are cuddly and cute, but if you see one in the woods alone (you think), "don't attempt to pet it, as mama bear is lurking around somewhere." At 6 weeks of age the cubs weigh about 2 pounds. When they are 2 months, the cubs leave the den with their mother for a learning experience and continue to nurse on their mother's rich in fat milk throughout the summer. Sometimes they den with their mother through the following winter. When leaving their mother, young bears may stay with their litter siblings through the second summer.

Bear Wearing Chap

By Lorie N. Thompson

He sat there just sitting
with style and flair.
He sat there and smiled
with a bear in his hair.

One passerby pointed.
"There's a bear,
can't you see?
A bear in his hair,

now how can that be?"

Yet, still he sat on
with a bear on his cap.
He sat there just sitting,
that bear-wearing chap.

Mary Carlton stands by a mushroom shaped boulder in her yard. The original owner of the rock ranch, Mary is now deceased.

PRIM'S PHENOMENAL MYSTERY

The Sun Times
By Chastine E. Shumway

Authors Note: *People have asked me how I became interested in the Round Boulders of Prim, Arkansas. In 2002 Randy Kemp, Editor of The Sun Times gave me an assignment to do a story on the 'Round Rocks of Prim. He said, "I've always wanted to do it."*
Not knowing Randy, I thought, "rocks?" But this was my first assignment for 'The Sun Times'. Years ago my father who lived here took me fishing down there, but I never saw any round rocks. So away I went to California Mountain with pen and camera in hand. The people and the communities put a spell on me, and I have never been the same. I had been told it was a secluded, seldom visited group of communities and visitors were not wanted. But for some reason this did not bother willy-nilly me. Well I met Odis Hipp, Mary Carlton, Lillie (Thrasher) Stevens), who had owned the 'land of rocks' at one time or another. The Johnny Carltons welcomed me to the Prim Diner. Then Johnny Carlton toured me on the boulders in his truck with a running board. As he went over sharp rocks, through thick brush, rocky inclines I hid my eyes. He said, "Are you sick, Chris?"
I said, "No, I'm just scared to death." He showed me the Bluffs, and the wow-some boulders. From then on, I called him, "John Wayne of the Ozarks."

When I began writing my article, I thought I must contact the State Geologists. That's when Mike Howard and Doug Hanson came to Prim and became friends to all. The rest is history. Several articles were written for various newspapers and appeared on Channel 7 TV about the 'land of Prim' and the fabulous round boulders. Politicians came, teachers, school children, etc. The doors of California Mountain have been opened ever since, but the story on the boulders is not finished, there is more yet to come.

Yes readers, I am under a spell forever and everyone that sees them is under it too. By the way don't expect to purchase for décor. You can't even get them from rock companies. Odis Hipp and Mary Carlton were the only ones who sold them years back. Greg Wells and Lillie Stevens have thousands of boulders on their land. People have offered $1,000, but so far no buy!

The Moon Boulders

Much of the rocky land in the Arkansas Ozarks has little value, but in this rugged, deeply religious community in north Cleburne County is a wonderment of nature that has gone largely unnoticed over the centuries—the moon rocks of Prim.

There is an air of mystery surrounding these diamond-in-the-rough treasures.

Nature has strewed numerous astonishingly-round boulders over a fairly small area of a few acres. These 1,000–6,000 lb. boulders are of tannish color, most of them perfectly round and are embedded with deep lines. Their physical stony faces have been exposed to all kinds of weather. Some are textured with petrified green moss, creating a special characterized look. Some of the rocks have a flower growing out of its crevice. They definitely look as if they are related to the moon. In fact they have many characteristics of that celestial body.

Other boulders in this area take on other unusual shapes. Mary Carlton (since deceased) has two of these oddities in her yard. One is shaped just like a huge oblong peanut shell, and the other resembles a mushroom.

There are many tales and theories about how the rocks appeared. Carlton's Diner is the only restaurant in Prim and is a general hangout for the townspeople and visitors. It is 17 years old and is a place where the Prim locals and visitors relax and 'chew the fat' and eat the best hamburgers around. Joyce and John A. Carlton own the restaurant and have initiated many good things for this community, including a library nook in the restaurant with donated books lining the shelves and a ballpark for the kids.

Visiting the diner, Mary Carlton's name was mentioned. It seems that she had just sold one of her round rocks from her farm for $300. A friend of hers speculated that she should have gotten $1,000.

Local hearsay is that perhaps the boulders came from outer space—meteorites shaped into roundness by a rapidly-spinning, fiery flight through the heavens. Other speculation says that they are of volcanic nature, rounded off like cannon balls when they whirled upward through the mouth of an erupting fissure.

Still others insist they must be king-sized "geodes"—nodules of stone common to Uruguay, Brazil, certain regions of the western United States and other areas. But geodes, besides being much smaller than these rocks of up to four-foot or more in diameter, have a center of crystals or mineral matter. These rocks are solid, not hollow.

"These are Martians in disguise, and we better act as if we don't know it and just leave them alone," one Prim youngster cautioned this reporter.

Odis Hipp, a knowledgeable previous landowner of the unique rocks, has told the story about one lady who wrote him from Maine and wanted him to send her a rock parcel post. Jokingly he said, "I should've sent her the one that weighed 4,000 pounds—COD."

Hipp also tells of a letter he received from a woman in Pennsylvania. "These rocks of yours are a Heaven-Sent omen of the beginning of the end of the Earth. Erosion did not bring your boulders into view—the Creator did!"

Hipp said, "I'm sure not going to touch that one."

But here's one tale that is interesting, and some of it is true. Prior to the Osage Treaty of 1808, the first humans to settle in this virgin timbered area were the Osage Indians who revered these unique rocks. It has been said that they traded these monstrous rocks to explorers for much wampum. But there was a catch. Without modern conveniences, they were unmovable. The reluctant explorer, sweaty and worn to a frazzle had to move on without his treasure. As he disappeared into the sunset, the Indian chief watched him go while he sat on the boulder counting his wampum and puffing contentedly on his pipe waiting for the next big deal!

No matter where they are from, centuries have passed, and the magnificent rocks are still standing. These mystifying round rocks have increased in value, so "thar's gold in these hills."

On May 23, 1992 the community celebrated its 100th anniversary with a parade. The late Gov. Orville Faubus served as the Parade Marshal. J. B. Hunt, the trucking magnate who had grown up in Prim was there too, hobnobbing with all of his hometown friends. A parade with seven floats rolled down the street.

Odis Hipp manned a red truck with a float decorated in America's patriotic colors of red, white, and blue. On its decorated flat bed rode two guests of honor—'the round rocks of Prim.'

In 1963, when the late Theodore Carlton owned this 10-acre tract full of round boulders, an Arkansas Geological Commission team headed by Dr. Thomas Freeman contacted him and undertook a cursory investigation in 1964, but the investigation did not allow time for elaborate study and determination of their complete stratigraphic and geographic distribution.

Dr. Freeman said the spheroid boulders appeared "in all stages of being liberated from the parent formation." He estimated the round sandstone rocks to be as much as 300 million years old and they were more than likely formed through an iron-oxidation process. The high iron content in the sandstone caused the hardening of a shell-like casing, which was tougher than surrounding rock being formed around it. When erosion later took place, according to the geological commission's aptly-named Charles Stone, the iron cement protected the round centers, while the softer rock around them crumbled away.

"This is a spheroidal-weathering process, as we call it," said Stone. "Spheroidal weathering gradually works toward roundness." Rocks similar to these elsewhere "are not as spectacular or unique as the ones in Prim or the Greers Ferry Lake area," he said.

All recent inquiries in Prim about the rocks brought the comment, "Odis Hipp is the person who can tell you all about the rocks."

Visiting with the tall well-versed man was interesting. If 61-year-old Odis Hipp's dream ever materializes, and these out-of-the-world objects are promoted right, Prim will be one of the most sought-after vacation spots in Arkansas.

Hipp, a Cleburne County businessman, bought the property from Theodore Carlton. As a boy Hipp had always held a fascination for the round rocks. As he grew to manhood and married his childhood sweetheart, Joyce Thomas, there was not much time for anything but making a living for his family. Due to having his fingers in several pots, he could only dream and visualize about what he would like to do with the rocks. One recurring dream was to make a park for others to enjoy-a 'Round Rock Park.' An admission would be charged for the upkeep of the park. It would give local people jobs and a sanctuary where nature studies could be done by groups of students, and an area where tourists could see Prim's abundant wild deer, turkeys, eagles, and of course the round rocks. In his mind he sees rocks and tree stumps as picnic tables, displays of other rocks for rock hounds and pebble hounds, postcards featuring Prim and the rocks, and on and on. One of the rocks that interests him has a hole through it. This could be used as a fountain with the water squirting out of it. The land, which he no longer owns, has an endless spring. It still meanders throughout the mighty oaks and pines and the shaggy hickory trees. And throughout this land the mighty rocks lay as mysterious sentinels bearing an unsolved, perhaps even sacred, secret.

Hipp is a builder and raises beef cattle. He's been known to get his pick and shovel out and dig up rocks just to see how big they were. "If you see any of them in other places, it is because they have been brought from Prim," he said. "Nobody ever paid much attention to these rocks around here. They have just been part of our heritage, I guess."

One day he brought one rock up to his backyard. It lay there for a long time before Don Lafferty of Heber Springs saw it and asked to buy it. That started the rock business rolling. "I sold it and four more to him for $5 apiece." Hipp has sold quite a few of the rocks since, priced at $50 and up. People have bought them for their rock gardens and decorative purposes. Some have bought them to decorate tourist attractions like Farwell Dinosaur Park near Eureka Springs and the Natural Bridge at Clinton.

"One day some people drove up to my home in a black Lincoln. The man asked me, 'Are you the man with the round rocks?' I nodded my head, yes. "Well I'd like to look at them." The man was Gerald K. Smith who owns the park where the Christ of the Ozarks stands. He was buying it to place it at the entrance of the "Christ of the Ozarks" statue in Eureka Springs. The rock is billed as "The Rock of Ages." He paid $250 for it.

Several of his rocks are found at the entrance to Nixon Park at Edgemont, a town on the shores of Greers Ferry Lake.

He has also sold some to the Eden Isle resort development near Heber Springs for $185each.

Scratching his head, he says, "No tellin' how many of these rocks are still under the ground. I believe there are more round stones beneath the surface." Hipp remembers the day he saw the rounded tip of a rock emerging from the ground. He became obsessed with digging it up without harming it. With pick and shovel in hand he worked day and night. The more he toiled the more he saw that it was the most perfect round rock he had ever seen. When he finally uncovered it, he decided to display it in his front yard. He built a sled, putting this monstrous rock on it. It was so heavy that the slats on the sled bent. With an old Ford 8N tractor he slowly hauled it to the front lawn. In later years he moved the rocks with a 6000-pound capacity lift and a winch truck.

He enjoys visiting and touring people, but lots of time is involved doing this, and it costs him money and time from his business. "There would be a good tour business for someone in this area," he speculated.

The Stevens, who bought this land from Hipp, are good people. When anyone visits this lady with the winsome smile, she gladly tours people through the rocks on her property. Her nickname is "Thrasher."

"It's not unusual to see students studying these rocks to write their thesis," she said. "Even photographers with the latest zoom or digital camera equipment have taken pictures to put calendars together. The last photographer was going to send me a calendar but he never did."

As far as you can see, there are round rocks throughout a certain area of the land. Walking over to one huge rock, she said, as she placed her hand on it, "We've owned this ranch for 30 years. The tips of some of these round rocks were only showing a little when we moved here. Now look at this one. The theory is that the earth trembles and the abundant seeping waters of Arkansas have stirred the earth's crust, turning these rocks into oval shapes."

Researching the story of the round rocks, it was discovered that there had been no scientific study since the quick investigation 38 years ago. But a personal invitation to William V. Bush, director of the Arkansas Geology

Commission, to make the 80-mile drive north from Little Rock for a new look was warmly accepted.

"A team of geologists, he said, would be honored to come in the fall when the bugs are hibernating."

State Geologist Begin Study

Monday, October 28, 2005, was a foggy, somewhat cool morning in Prim, but none of the more than 300 people noticed as they excitedly crammed themselves into Carlton's Diner.

Why this excitement?

Well, the big day had arrived. The state geologists from Little Rock were on their way to study the phenomenon of the round "moon rocks" unique to this whisper of a community on the Cleburne—Stone county line.

The diner was decorated with newspaper articles about the round rocks, and welcome ads from the local businesses. Everyone was greeted with smiles and "hellos" from the Ladies Auxiliary with plates of donuts and colorful Halloween treats, and nut bread donated by Sue Davis of the Greers Ferry Sweet Donut Shop and laden trays of various cookies made by the Prim women. Joyce Carlton, owner of the diner, served coffee and Kool-Aid furnished by The Family Market and Razorback Grocery stores of Greers Ferry.

There was lots of comradeship among the men talking about the big-racked buck that got away, and of course, politics. Several dignitaries and business people mingled, including Sheriff Dudley Lemon, Judge Claude Dill, and Bob Bogard, an area Realtor.

Roger Hipp, Social Studies teacher at Fox Rural Special School and Jeff Stanley, the Science/Biology teacher of West Side School brought two busloads of 8th, 9th, 10, and 11th grade children to enjoy the once-in-a-lifetime educational experience. Between the chattering and the drowning gales of laughter from the school children, Jeff Stanley tried to calm them down a little. The atmosphere was like an 'ageless never-land' where no one ever grows up. Flash bulbs began popping as Mike Howard and William (Doug) Hanson, the two geologists, walked in. Doug had a large box in his hands. The Arkansas State Geologist Commission sent small packages of Arkansas rocks with information about the rocks enclosed, which everyone received.

Odis Hipp, a well-known builder and previous owner of the land of boulders knew they were coming to inspect, stood up and introduced the geologists and thanked Joyce Carlton for opening the restaurant on a Monday and for her help in organizing this day. He introduced Thrasher Stevens, who now owns the land of rocks. Plaques donated by Heber Springs Wal-Mart were given in appreciation to each Geologist for coming to do this study.

"Mikey" Howard, as he is called on the Internet, an accomplished geologist and published writer, talked about why they were doing the study. He and Doug Hanson answered questions from the rock hounds and pebble hounds and others in the crowd about the rocks.

After the down-to-earth ceremony, Thrasher Stevens, the owner of the property for 30 years said, "It's time to go to the Ranch of the Rocks."

With scientific tools in hand the jaunty geologists headed down to the land of the mysterious boulders, accompanied by throngs of children who jumped out of the buses and scampered through the woods.

Looking at the rocks, Mike said, "These are sedimentary rocks. They are solid all the way through." Doug pointed to a fracture through one boulder and used his measuring stick while Mike took pictures with his digital camera. "An acorn will fall in that fracture one of these days, and a tree will grow in the middle," he predicted.

Two boys, Cory Snearly and Lee Dobrzeniecki from Westside School had trouble seeing over the crowd and hopped on a boulder, getting a birdseye view of the geologists as they probed and measured.

Afterwards, Johnny Carlton (John Wayne of the Ozarks) took the geologists to Greg Wells' land, where there were rocks and more rocks. Some were completely round while others were in unique shapes. Greg Wells confided, "I'd like to give this peanut-shaped boulder to our previous President, Jimmy Carter, for his museum. He was one of the finest, most honorable Presidents we ever had in the United States."

After completing the tour of the rocks, Johnny Carlton took the geologist to visit the nearby Yellow Bluffs as the memorable day wound down. The visit ended with children and people bringing in Indian relics and fossils found in the Prim area. Mike and Doug were very interested in these objects that had survived, wholly or as pieces, from the past.

Now they were ready to take their data back to Little Rock and determine more about these unique boulders and update a 1964 geology report.

ROCKS OF AGES

Author's note: This article was written by my reporter friend, Christine Arpe Gang, and was published in the Commercial Appeal on November 16, 2004. It is used here by permission with pictures on the back book cover also published in the Commercial Appeal.)

For 32 years Lillie "Thrasher" Stevens has felt a connection with the round boulders that dot her property in this hamlet near the resort areas of Greers Ferry and Fairfield Bay.

"I feel like they are here for a purpose—that they are supposed to be here," Stevens said.

Residents of Prim, which is about 150 miles from Memphis, Tenn., have long been fascinated with the giant orbs of compressed sandstone that look like they've fallen from outer space. They have used them in their own landscaping, sometimes ringed with flowers, and as sentinels in front of public buildings such as the town's post office.

Three round boulders sit in front of Carlton's Diner, Prim's unofficial community center. Those who stop in for hamburgers and home cooking, including many vacation homeowners from Memphis and the Mid-South, are often intrigued by the rocks and want to see more.

"I always call Thrasher and ask her if she can show them," said Joyce Carlton, who owns the diner with her husband, John. "She loves the rocks and loves to show them if she's not busy."

To geologist Mike Howard, "Stevens's property is "the rock ranch. It's the area most concentrated with rocks," said Howard, who has been studying the formations along with his associate, William "Doug" Hanson, for about a year. They are both with the Arkansas Geological Commission.

So what exactly are the boulders some locals call "moon rocks" and how did they get here?"

Howard said, "It's for sure they did not fall from the sky. Their beginnings go back 300 million years when much of Arkansas was under sea water."

"This area was analogous to the Gulf of Mexico," Howard recently told some town people who had gathered in the diner to hear his report.

Over millions of years, the sand and shells on the ocean floor were buried under additional sediment such as sand, silt and clay. The heat and pressure generated by the layer of sediment caused the particles to cement and form rocks.

Erosion and weather worked on the formations until they turned into "spherical concretions."

Iron in the sandstone particles dots the boulders with orange flecks and preserves them in their round shape. Petrified mosses and lichens cover their jagged surfaces.

On one of their research trips to Prim, Howard and Hanson discovered the largest of the boulders so far, a rock 12 feet in diameter in a creek in a remote area.

Howard estimates there are several thousand spherical boulders in the region of Prim and to the south in White County around Bald Knob,

Although they haven't finished their study of the boulders, Howard and Hanson presented an educational poster on them to the Industrial Minerals Forum.

The geologists gave a copy of the poster to the people of Prim. The Carltons plan to mount it on a wall in the diner under a sheet of Plexiglass.

"The rocks are scarce but not rare," Howard said. "There are other examples of spherical concretions in Morocco, in Theodore Roosevelt National Park in North Dakota, on New Zealand's South Island, in Colorado, Utah and Wyoming and elsewhere around the world. The round rocks seem to regularly "pop" out of the ground on Steven's property. She hastens their exposure by pulling back leaves and soil from around the base of the newly discovered specimen."

"There are at least six more rocks than there were the last time I was here," said Hanson.

One rock that recently emerged knocked over a small tree growing on top of it.

"I've lived here for 32 years and there are at least 20 rocks that have come out of the ground in that time," said Stevens. "No telling how many are still in there."

She finds them when she rakes away leaves. Her dog exposed one while digging in the dirt.

Local folks call the spheres that are joined "peanuts."

Stevens would like to remove the trees around the rocks to hasten water runoff and erosion to expose them fully.

Her dream is to create a public park where people can come and view the rocks. "I'd like to see nature trails and picnic tables," she said. "But it will cost a lot of money."

She won't be raising money by selling boulders even though they command $400 to $1000 or more.

The geologists say the stones are marketable for several reasons: overall uniform spherically; sizes averaging 2 ½ to 3 ½ feet in diameter; and a compact form that makes them unlikely to break apart easily.

"The rocks are not only a scientific curiosity, they could be an economic benefit to the area with tourism or in selling them," Howard and Hanson wrote in their report.

But transporting boulders that weigh 3,500 pounds and more is risky.

Dereta Well's husband, Greg Wells, once tried to move a boulder by pushing it up a hill with a bulldozer.

"Halfway up the incline the boulder got loose, rolled off the bulldozer and crashed into the feed bin for the chicken house," Dereta Wells said. "That's why we don't move them very often. It's dangerous."

Joyce Carlton remembers a truck going off the road when the boulder it was carrying shifted.

The Wells property also has many round boulders, but they are near a creek about 2 miles from their house. The trail to the site is so rugged a four-wheel drive vehicle or an all terrain four-wheeler is needed to get there.

Many of the boulders are still embedded on a steep hill that rises on one side of the creek. Every million years or so erosion breaks one loose and sends it rolling toward the creek.

"I don't know why we don't find any (boulders) on the other side of the creek" Howard said during a foray to the site.

Because it is at the junction of five physiographic provinces, Arkansas is geologically diverse state. Diamonds and the "biggest and best" quartz crystals, and 2,500 caves are found in the state," said Hanson. "Prim's mysterious round boulders draw the curious.

"We're glad our town and the rocks are getting to be known," Joyce Carlton said. "We're proud of our little community"

Bob and Jill Stubbs owns this particular round rock.

Greg Wells, Johnny Carlton, Joyce Carlton, Odis Hipp, author Chastine
Shumway and Sun-Times Editor Randy Kemp listen to a presentation
given by the geologists.

Arkansas Geologists Mike Howard and Doug Hanson receive plaques from Prim in appreciation of their study.

On October 26, 2004, the weather was dreary and rainy, and a patchy fog hung over Greers Ferry Lake that you could slice with a knife. This did not deter the enthusiasm of the State Geologists from completing their planned mission to the beloved community of Prim. This was the day everyone had waited for, and another marvel was about to happen. This would be a historical day for the residents, their guests and their ghostly ancestry guest of yesteryear to remember.

Two years ago Geologists Mike Howard and Doug Hanson came as Professional State scientists to the Prim. What would bring these scientists from Little Rock to this whisper of a community, which consisted of a post office, hardware, a general store, fire station, and Carlton's Diner? They came to this community to study about the mysterious largest round boulders found in Prim. In this cautious community towards strangers, these men ended up as good friends to the hill people and school children of Prim.

Doug is a Staff Geologist with the agency and a Registered Professional Geologist in Arkansas. He is an experienced geologic mapper. He is a family man, with a wife and three daughters. He is also an Eagle Scout.

Mike is a Geology Supervisor and a Registered Professional Geologist in Arkansas. He answers mineral and economic mineral resource related questions from both industry and the public. He hosts a website, rock-houndingAR.com that is dedicated to the dispersal of information relating to collecting Arkansas minerals. He is the author of several state publications and a privately published book about Arkansas quartz crystal deposits. Both Mike and Doug lead field trips and make public presentations.

On the first of their visits to study these boulders, they gave out packages of Arkansas rocks to teachers and students and townspeople. They took many pictures of the round boulders and the unusual shapes that occurred in the boulders when they strayed from their parent rock.

Unbeknownst to the people of Prim, behind the scenes, Mike and Doug were making a huge wall size poster to spread the word about these interesting boulders to the mineralogists who attended the National Geography meeting. The meeting was held at the University of Memphis Conference Center in Memphis, Tennessee. They named this awesome poster

"Prim's Unique Spherical Boulders." The poster caused quite a stir among the mineralogist from all over the country. Several of the mineralogist asked, "Where is Prim?" After this meeting, Doug and Mike decided that the only place for this wall-sized poster was 'the land of Prim'.

Instead of a study they decided to present the poster to Prim at Carlton's Diner.

Representative Bill Stovall was the guest of honor and speaker for this morning gathering. Everything eventually calmed down and Bill introduced the State Geologists from Little Rock.

Mike Howard and Doug Hanson presented the wall-sized poster with large bold letters, which said, 'PRIM'S UNIQUE SPHERICAL BOULDERS' to the community of Prim. Underneath that heading there was a paragraph about these remarkable phenomenon's. You must make a trip to the diner in Prim to see this piece of history. No words can describe it.

Christine Gang, a reporter of The Commercial Appeal of Memphis, Tenn. came with a photographer to attend the presentation of the poster. Also in attendance was Brian Haile who was running for Cleburne County sheriff. Now it was time for the guests to go on a tour of the rocks. Hopping in the jeeps and 4-wheelers, this procession was off and running!

The tour included the Johnny Stevens land of round rocks, the Greg Wells acres of boulders (Sugar Creek), and other Prim resident's ornate yard display of these rocks. Thrasher Stevens has a dream of starting a rock park. Since word has spread about these fabulous boulders, several clubs and individuals have called her wanting to tour these strange boulders. Thrasher is preparing to have a Rock Park someday to share these gifts of nature with the public.

Mrs. Greg Wells (Dereta Wells) assisted the geologists in touring the guests in her jeep. Her grandson, Hayden Lay rode with her. Norette Underwood and another guest rode with Dereta on the tour. Norette is a veterinarian in Trumann and owns the Trumann Animal Clinic. She said, "I think the rocks are fascinating and I had to come for this occasion."

Dereta was very adept in driving her jeep through the many round rock wooded areas. She guided the jeep over sharp rocks and climbed the steep grades of the hills. The Well's have 20 acres of these unique rocks. Sugar

Camp is jam packed with round boulders and this property is a scientists delight. At the end of the tour, Dereta took them to their log cabin over-looking a gorgeous view. On this property there are also unusual shaped rocks, which have been parented from the round rocks.

Meanwhile, back at the Diner Joyce was busy showing town's people the poster, and preparing food for the return of the touring group.

The Carlton's are going to have the poster covered in a plexi-glass and it will be mounted on the Diner's history walls until a community center is built. This valuable poster belongs to all of the people of Prim.

MYSTERY UNFOLDS OF ROUND BOULDERS

The phenomenally round boulders unique to this rugged community have yielded some of their secrets. But the pair of state geologists studying the "Moon rocks" were so impressed with fossils and artifacts presented to them by community members that they are planning yet another trip in the spring.

Mike Howard and Doug Hanson, representing the Arkansas Geological Commission, began their study of the odd round rocks in late October 2002, starting with a tour of Thrasher Stevens property and the Greg Wells place, where there were thousands of boulders. As far as anyone knew, this was virgin territory covered with timber and rocks and springs and had not been studied before. It is almost impassable with rough and hilly terrain, but engrossing to the geologists. They returned December 10th when area resident Johnny Carlton also took them to the history-laden Yellow Bluffs to see the beautiful rock formations there.

In the 1800s the bluffs were a favorite campsite for many outlaws including Jesse James, and the Sinclair boys who camped out there and hid their stolen gold in that area. In fact there are a couple of outlaws who are buried beneath the rocks. Many a treasure hunter has searched for the hidden wealth in these bluffs but to no avail. On one of the bluff shelters the geologists found where a bear had bedded down. The geologists laughed as they said, "We were thankful that he had gone elsewhere to visit for the day. The surface of this land is not only covered with these valuable boulders, there are a great more beneath the surface. When we were in college, we learned to read the rocks like we read books. The surface and inside of rocks tell us many things. There is much to be studied here. We are not finished with our study. We want to bring another scientist with us here to investigate the area where the fossils and artifacts have been found too."

So, what secrets have been extracted from the study of the rocks so far? Below is the text of their preliminary synopsis of the Prim boulders, written by the two geologists:

SYNOPSIS OF ROUND BOULDERS
By Geologists Doug Hanson and Mike Howard

The area in and around Prim, Arkansas is underlain by units of sandstone and shale that were deposited in a delta-like environment some 300 million years ago (a). Geologists term the rock units as the Bloyd/Yale Formations and consider them of Morrowan age. The deposition of these sediments was on a relatively flat plain that sloped gently to the south. Rivers built deltas out into the ocean and deposited their sediments in a system of different deposits typical of what is now observed at the mouth of the present day Mississippi River.

The sediments were buried by overlaying materials and eventually compressed and cemented to become the rock units we now observe. Since the end of the Paleozoic, around 245 Ma, the region has been exposed to weathering and erosion. This action, along with the relative resistance of certain rock units, has resulted in the present day topography of the region. The origin of the spherical boulders at Prim is related to several geological processes and the vast amount of geological time involved. When viewed in outcrop, the boulders are seen in every state of release from the host sandstone: from spherical masses embedded in the host rock, to loose accumulations of residual stones downslope from the host interval, and even to those that have reached creek level and been moved downstream by high water flow. At one newly reported site of a church, the entire sandstone unit has weathered to loose sandy soil that contains residual spherical boulders. It is now recognized that there are several local sandstone units in the region that are the sources of the Prim boulders. Similar processes have affected each of these units to allow the formation of the spherical stones.

The process of formation probably began with the solution of calcite-bearing materials in the sedimentary units sometime shortly after deposition and compaction, and the nucleation and growth of the dissolved calcite in restricted sandstone beds. We have not observed deformed spherical boulders, so the sediments must have already been compacted before cementation began. These beds are usually 3 to 6 feet in thickness and are typically underlain and overlain by high-energy sand deposits displaying crossbedding features. The host sandstone is generally featureless on exposure, but portions of the unit, when thicker, may display honeycombed solution-related texture.

After the initial growth of the cementation, the movement of groundwater carrying dissolved iron through the host rock started an additional cementation that resulted in some iron-oxide bands and often limonite-goethite case hardening of many of the presently loose boulders.

Erosion of the host sandstone slowly removes the rock face on outcrop, and the cemented boulders are left as positive features. They survive the loss of host rock due to their superior cementation, and when freed, eventually move downslope from the outcrop face, finally reaching creek level. This type of gravity-driven system of downslope movement is called mass wasting and is generally more active in drier climates then presently exist in Arkansas. Greater vegetation cover holds the underlying soil and loose material in place, due to presence of a root matte and litter cover that slows the run off of water. It is probable that many of the boulders reached their present positions slow the run off of water. It is probable that many of the boulders reached their present positions some 10 thousands years ago when much of Arkansas was climatically much drier than today. Several features of the Prim boulders are aesthetically pleasing and therefore, make them marketable as decorator stones.

Their overall uniform sphericity.

Their size, most ranging from 2.5 to 3.5 feet in diameter.

Their compactness. This property prevents them from being broken during transport.

Their uniqueness to the building and yard decoration trades.

Only small concrete spheres and glass globes to about 15 inches in diameter are available to the general public.

There appears to be as many as several thousand of these spherical boulders in the region of Prim and for a short distance to the south into Cleburne County. However, only a small percentage may be recoverable for decorator stone, simply due to the roughness of the local terrain.

Concentrations may be available for machine extraction at some sites, but many are present widely scattered on steep slopes off the cress of local hillsides. These boulders would require more old time skills, like use of mules and skidders, similar to early logging efforts in the region. For such boulders, the cost of recovery would result in a higher price than those machines extracted.

The question is always asked, "Just what are they worth?" The answer is simple: whatever the market will bear. Because the boulders are scare and somewhat difficult to recover, and because they are unique, when a potential buyer becomes interested and decides they must have one, the process of determining what the seller can get, is somewhat similar to the situation of purchasing a new car. The buyer can set a price with the possibility of coming down, and a potential buyer can make an offer for a given stone.

Until recently, pricing was more a guessing game, but as these stones get better known and demand builds, the pricing will reach a point where a few sell to those buyers who are convinced that they must have one or more of these stones. Comments heard our trips to Prim include present prices in the range from $400 to $800 each for the more spherical easily accessed stones."

THE AUTHOR

Chastine Shumway is an author who has worn coats of many colors. She gives God the credit HE has given her in writing. The writing bug hit her when her first story won an award in high school and was read on the radio. After she married articles about her children appeared in many magazines. She has been editor of several newspapers; *The Whitehaven Star, The Southaven News, Teen Scenes and Family Scenes (which she created and owned)*. Elvis Presley wrote the sendoff article for the first Teen Scenes paper. There were many visits to Graceland after that happening. Later she started a Personnel Agency in Memphis. All of a sudden everyone needed a resume in order to get a good job, so she began writing her client's resumes for free to go to the positions she sent them on. They were getting such good results that her business boomed. She had to start charging for cover letters and resumes. She spent her personal time giving speeches to clubs and appearing on TV and radio programs. Then someone tacked, "The Resume Lady" on her. Schools and colleges had her to speak at their graduations. She met with panels of college professors on TV to discuss her expertise and secret in writing extraordinary cover letters and resumes for her clients that got their foot in the door. Her resume business was getting 99% results. She was the first resume writer to use colored paper, which was a "no no" in writing resumes at that time. She said, the 'Cover Letter' whets the employer's appetite. She was known to have an unbelievable insight of people, and as 'The Resume Lady' was able to put their personalities on paper. Someone in England visiting America came to her and got the job they were looking for.

Meanwhile she was driving a sparkly gold Continental, a surprise gift from her husband Wil, with a license plate that read 'The Resume Lady'. When she drove down the street, people honked their horns, stopping traffic and asking her about the resumes. When she came out of TV and radio stations, people were crowded around her car asking for her autograph and making appointments. One day when her husband came home she had been crying. He asked her what was wrong. She said, "I feel I'm something I'm not." He immediately sold the business with her menu, and three owners since have purchased the business."

Her most treasured jewels are her family of six children, grandchildren and great grandchildren. Her oldest daughter Sandy died of cancer two years ago. Her husband, Will passed away at their 50th wedding anniversary celebration. Chris, as she is called now, loves people, enjoys researching and writing historical articles for magazines and newspapers. She started a Writer's Club in Memphis, Tennessee at the Zanzadu Book Store. There were never enough seats to be had. She wrote a fiction book called Ayoka's Prophecy, which was published in 2004. It is a spellbound and tension building adventure of the Western Plains in the 1800s. In her spare time she enjoys reading the National Geography magazine and listening to the history channel on TV. Her great Uncle Julius Frederick who was a survivor of 'The Greely Expedition is in history books. She belongs to a Scrabble Club, enters cooking and writing contests. She has one published children's story, which was published by SIRS, available for school libraries nation wide called *An Unusual Horse*. This is an immense honor. This same story has been sold three times. She attends writing conferences throughout the Southern States, one of her favorite being held at Ole Miss College, and has completed a study on 'Writing to Sell Fiction' from the well-known Writer's digest School and is working on her third book now.

God, her family and friends play an immeasurable role in her life. What messages does this 77-year old woman give to her readers? "It's never too late to follow your dream. I'm proof of it!"

BOOK ACKNOWLEDGEMENTS

Debra Baker
Bob Bogard, Realtor
Wanda Biggs
Wm. V. Bush, Director AR Geological Comm.
Joyce and Johnny Carlton, Carlton's Diner
Jason Carlton
Mary Carlton (deceased), original owner of boulders
Carpenter Computer Service
Zac Cothren, Head Librarian of Cleburne County Library
Myra Chapen
Janet Clary retired librarian, Of Cleburne County Library
Mickey Barnett, Historian
Charles Stuart, President of Historical Center
FL and Cleta Davis
Sue Davis
Judge Claude Dill
Freda Dillard
Game & Fish Ecologist, Rick Eastridge
Carl Garner
Jean Garner
Georgie's Florist
Rex Harral
Roger Hipp, Social Studies Teacher Fox Rural Special School
Sheriff Dudley Lemon

Patti Upton

Edgemont Postmaster Sharon Nelson and crew

Mel LaVier & Becky Everett

Bobby Smith, Greers Ferry Postmaster

Peggy Harris, Aromatique

Odis and Joyce Hipp

Beth and Tim Janssen

David Lee, Publisher, The Sun Times

Randy Kemp, Editor, The Sun Times

Lorie Thompson, News Editor, The Sun Times

Little Rock State Geologists, Mike Howard and Doug Hanson

Mike Melvin

David Morris

Mayor Bob Paschall, deceased

Jo Price, Heber Springs Area Chamber of Commerce

Judy Roberson, Christian Book Store

Richard Shumway,

Arthur Shumway,

Sandra Shumway Jukkola (deceased),

Susan Shumway Brummett

Florence Shumway Dixon,

Betty Shumway Franklin

Jeff Stanley, Science/Biology teacher, West Side School

Johnny and Lillie Stevens, Prim Rock Park Owners

Jan Stratton, hair stylist

Rep. Bill Stovall

Ernestine Stubbs

Jill Stubbs, Prim School Teacher

Verner Stubbs

Glynda Turley

Darlene Thomas, Prim Postmaster
Gregg & Dereta Wells, Owner of boulder farm
U.S. Army Corps of Engineers, Little Rock District
Jean Stark retired librarian, Of Greers Ferry Branch Library
Jerry Davis

There are many others that I'm sure I have missed, but my thanks are to all of you

978-0-595-44633-9
0-595-44633-7

Printed in the United States
97525LV00002B/262-309/A